Prayers
That
Attract

Divine
Help from

Heaven

Your Spiritual Prayer Arrows

PASTOR ISRAEL A. OLUWAGBEMIGA

WESTBOW
P R E S S®
A DIVISION OF THOMAS NELSON
& ZONDERVAN

WestBow Press books may be ordered through booksellers or by contacting:

WestBow Press
A Division of Thomas Nelson & Zondervan
1663 Liberty Drive
Bloomington, IN 47403
www.westbowpress.com
1 (866) 928-1240

ISBN: 978-1-5127-8728-3 (sc)
ISBN: 978-1-5127-8730-6 (hc)
ISBN: 978-1-5127-8729-0 (e)

Library of Congress Control Number: 2017907878

Print information available on the last page.

WestBow Press rev. date: 06/05/2017

for without holiness, no man shall
see God. Hebrew 12:14

Dedication

Firstly, I dedicate this prayer book to the Almighty God the father, the Son and the Holy Spirit, who has been my rock and faithful in all situation.

Then, to all the great men of God, I have been opportuned to have sat under as a student in the school of Deliverance and spiritual warfare, also as minister of the gospel of our Lord Jesus Christ. They have all in one way or the other impacted my life through the power of the Holy Ghost and their great ministration of the word of God. To the likes of Late Pa T.O Obadare of CAC, Pa Ojo Oluyi of CAC, Pastor Olusegun Ojo CAC, Pastor E.A. Adeboye of Redeemed Christian Church of God, Pastor Idowu Aminu of Pure Fire Miracles Ministries International (who beleived in me as a young preacher in those days); and finally to my dearest father in the Lord, Dr. D.K. Olukoya of Mountain of Fire and Miracles Ministries, under who's ministry, I have been able to understand so much about spiritual warfare and delivance battles for this present age.

Acknowledgement

Firstly, I will want to give thanks to the almighty God, for His love, knowledge, wisdom and understanding to be able to write this spiritual prayer arrow book.

To my beloved wife and children, Sister Beatrice, Jemima, Kezia and Miracle Oluwagbemiga, who have been so supportive and inspirational to the great call of God upon my life; I say thank you. I really appreciate you all and I pray, that, the Lord God Almighty will continue to reward you, in Jesus name.

To my late Parent Mr & Mrs S.F. Oduwole, My beloved brother (Oluwaseyi), my Sisters and brother in-laws (Mr. Esechie, Mr. Onatunde and Pastor Omojola (MFM), thank you for all your Love and support in one way or the other.

Then, to my late father in-law (Pa. D.O Uwagbai), my mother in-law (Mrs. E.O Uwagbai), The Adekunles and the Okorosobos; your encouragement, love and kind support can not be forgotten. Thank You.

To the entire member of Christ The Hope Of Glory Mission International, I really appreciate you all, for your love, support and cooperation, you accorded me during this period. The blessings of the Lord shall be your portions in Jesus name.

Finally, my thanks goes to the West Bow Press family for their great support in all aspect in the publication of this prayer book. God Bless you all.

Table of Contents

Introduction

Prayer that attract divine help from Heaven, are deep spiritual warfare prayers that have been written to help those who are tired of satanic attacks that has been confronting them, without knowing how to deal with them or what kind of prayers to pray. This prayer booklet is designed to target specific issues releated to our daily lives and it is A Do It Yourself Warfare Prayers.

It is a fact, that, as long as we are on the surface of this earth and we are truthly born again, we shall constantly be attacked and oppressed by the powers of darkness, according to the word of God; **And the dragon was enraged with the woman, and he went to make war with the rest of her offspring, who keep the commandments of God and have the testimony of Jesus Christ** (Revelation 12:17). But the good news is that, we shall surely overcome, so long as we can pray the right prayers and also possibly fast. There are some issues of life that sure need fasting. **However this kind goeth not out but by prayer and fasting** (Matthew 17:21).

How to use the book

The things you need to do before you start to pray the prayer points:

1. Examine yourself and settle yourself with God, if you know you are living in sin. You must surrender your life to Jesus Christ period.

2. Locate the area of your life that is troubled and needs deliverance, then, select the right prayer in this prayer book that address the issue.

3. Do the bible reading / confession in each prayer topic aggressively

4. Pray the prayers aggressively until some thing happen,
   - You can pray the prayers at night, 12am to 3am
   - You can pray them with fasting (Do this as your strength takes you)
   - You can take each prayer topic as long as you want 3days, 5days or 7days

5. During your prayer program, please try as much as possible to live a Holy life.

Destroying the Rod of the Wicked

Bible Reading and Confession

For the rod of the wicked shall not rest upon the lot of the righteous; lest the righteous put forth their hands unto iniquity. (Psalm 125:3)

For the Lord will have mercy on Jacob, and will yet choose Israel, and set them in their own land: and the strangers shall be joined with them, and they shall cleave to the house of Jacob. And the people shall take them, and bring them to their place: and the house of Israel shall possess them in the land of the Lord for servants and handmaids: and they shall take them captives, whose captives they were; and they shall rule over their oppressors. And it shall come to pass in the day that the Lord shall give thee rest from thy sorrow, and from thy fear, and from the hard bondage wherein thou waste made to serve, That thou shalt take up this proverb against the king of Babylon, and say, How hath the oppressor ceased! the golden city ceased! The Lord hath broken the staff of the wicked, and the sceptre of the rulers. (Isaiah 14:1–5)

Praise and Worship

Prayer Points

1. Rod of the wicked preventing my life from entering into my rest, break to pieces, by the power in the blood of Jesus.

2. Rod of the wicked resting on my marriage, break to pieces, by the power in the blood of Jesus.

3. I command the rod of the wicked, to rest upon the head of the wicked, in the name of Jesus.

4. Any power pointing evil rod at me or any member of my household, die, in the name of Jesus.

5. Rod of the wicked scattering my blessings, break to pieces, in the name of Jesus.

6. I command every occultic rod present in my family, preventing the children born to this family from shinning, break, in the name of Jesus.

7. Rod of sickness and frustration pointing at me, break, by the power in the blood of Jesus.

8. Any damage done to my life by any evil rod, break, in the name of Jesus.

9. Every rod of disappointment and failure, fashioned against me, break, in the name of Jesus.

10. Any power troubling my life with an evil rod, die, in the name of Jesus.

11. Any evil rod pointing to the heavenlies, to block my heavens, break, in the name of Jesus.

12. Any evil rod flogging me at night, break, in the name of Jesus.

13. Any witchcraft rod causing problem for me at the edge of my breakthrough, break, in the name of Jesus.

14. I decree, the rod of the wicked shall not rest upon my lot, in the name of Jesus.

15. I break any satanic rod of untimely death pointing at me, in the name of Jesus.

16. Rod of the wicked targeting my home break, in the name of Jesus.

17. I command, satanic rod of the wicked scattering my finances, break, in the name of Jesus.

18. I decree, the rod of the wicked shall not rest on my head or that of my children, in the name of Jesus.

19. My head, hear the word of the living God, you shall not obey any satanic instruction from any evil rod, in the name of Jesus.

20. I decree, the rod of the wicked shall not rest on the head of my children, in the name of Jesus.

21. O Lord, I thank you for answered prayer, in the name of Jesus.

Bible Reading and Confession

And they overcame him by the blood of the Lamb, and by the word of their testimony; and they loved not their lives unto the death. (Revelation 12:11)

Praise and Worship

Prayer Points

1. Blood of Jesus, fight for me, in the name of Jesus.
2. Whenever my name is being mentioned for evil, blood of Jesus answer them, in the name of Jesus.
3. Blood of Jesus, speak better things into my life, in the name of Jesus.
4. I destroy every satanic agenda / plan for my life, with the blood of Jesus, in the name of Jesus.
5. I receive my testimony today, by the power in the blood of Jesus.
6. Blood of Jesus, form a protective shield around me, in the name of Jesus.
7. Satan, I overcome you today, by the power in the Blood of Jesus.
8. I use the blood of Jesus to flush out of my life every demonic deposit in my blood stream, in the name of Jesus.
9. Blood of Jesus, begin to cry against every enemy of my life and physical existence, in the name of Jesus.

10. I lift-up the blood of Jesus, as a weapon of destruction against household wickedness, in the name of Jesus.
11. I use the blood of Jesus, to claim back all my lost fertile ground in the possession of the enemy, in the name of Jesus.
12. O Lord, I thank you for answered prayers, in Jesus name.

Anointing for Spiritual Growth

Bible Reading and Confession: 2 Corinthians 6

Verily, verily, I say unto you, Except a corn of wheat fall into the ground and die, it abideth alone: but if it die, it bringeth forth much fruit. (John 12:24)

Praise and Worship

Prayer Points

1. O Lord, give me the power to be faithful in my calling, in the name of Jesus.
2. I receive the anointing to remain steadfast, committed and consistent in my ministerial assignment, in the name of Jesus.
3. O Lord, give me the heart of a servant, so that, I can experience your blessings every day, in the name of Jesus.
4. I receive power to mount up with wings as eagle, in the name of Jesus.
5. I will not waste my calling, in the name of Jesus.
6. I declare war against spiritual ignorance in my life, in the name of Jesus.
7. I bind and cast out every unteachable spirit in my life, in the name of Jesus.
8. O Lord, break me down and remold me, to fit your purpose, in the name of Jesus.
9. I destroy every spiritual blockage, in my spiritual life, in the name of Jesus.

10. O Lord, fill me afresh with your power, in the name of Jesus.

11. I decree, my spiritual eyes shall not go dimmed, in the name of Jesus.

12. Spirit of worldliness, you shall not destroy my calling, die, in the name of Jesus.

13. Power of God, come into me and lift me above spiritual errors, in the name of Jesus.

14. Powers that ruin great men of God at their prime, you shall not locate me, die, in the name of Jesus.

15. I receive power like in the days of Pentecost, in the name of Jesus.

16. I receive divine immunity against any form of spiritual weakness, in the name of Jesus.

17. Powers monitoring me in-order to pull me down, loose control and die, in the name of Jesus.

18. I receive the anointing of ease that is in the blood of Jesus, in the name of Jesus.

19. Power of God to see and hear clearly form the throne of grace, possess me now, in the name of Jesus.

20. Thank you, Lord Jesus for answered prayers, in the name of Jesus.

Deliverance from the Spirit of Kadesh Barnea (Spirit of Stagnancy)

Bible Reading and Confession: Deuteronomy 13

Praise and Worship

Prayer Points

1. I refuse to stay at Kadesh-Barnea, I receive the power to enter my promise land, in the name of Jesus.
2. Powers of Kadesh-Barnea, attacking my divine Journey in life, die, in the name of Jesus.
3. Powers that want to waste me at Kadesh-Barnea, die, in the name of Jesus.
4. Satanic authority keeping me at Kadesh-Barnea, die, in the name of Jesus.
5. O Lord, move me forward by fire, in the name of Jesus.
6. Spirit of diversion at Kadesh-Barnea, loose your hold over my life, in the name of Jesus.
7. Powers calling my head to error, die, in the name of Jesus.
8. Powers making me to take a wrong turn in life, die, in the name of Jesus.
9. O Lord, seek me out from the multitude for uncommon breakthrough, in the name of Jesus.
10. My Father, put me back on the right path, in the name of Jesus.
11. Blood of Jesus, buy me back, where ever I have been sold to, in the name of Jesus.

12. I shall not be stagnant in the journey of life, in the name of Jesus.

13. I refuse to remain at the same spot in life, in the name of Jesus.

14. Powers responsible for lateness to the place of my miracles, die, in the name of Jesus.

15. Powers of Kadesh-Barnea, making me to make mistake in my journey, die, in the name of Jesus.

16. Powers responsible for rise and fall in my life, die, in the name of Jesus.

17. Spirit of time wastage, you will not waste my time, release me and die, in the name of Jesus.

18. I call forth the power of God, that made the heavens and the earth, take me out of this location, to where I should be now in life, in the name of Jesus.

19. Household wickedness causing obstacles for me on my way to my promise land, die, in the name of Jesus.

20. O Lord, I thank you for answered prayers, in Jesus name.

Power against the Evil Woman and Her Basket

Bible Reading and Confession

Then the angel that talked with me went forth, and said unto me, Lift up now thine eyes, and see what is this that goeth forth. And I said, what is it? And he said, this is an ephah that goeth forth. He said moreover, this is their resemblance through all the earth. And, behold, there was lifted up a talent of lead: and this is a woman that sitteth in the midst of the ephah. And he said, this is wickedness. And he cast it into the midst of the ephah; and he cast the weight of lead upon the mouth thereof. (Zechariah 5:5–8)

Praise and Worship

Prayer Points

1. Powers operating in this country / city from any satanic basket, die, in the name of Jesus.
2. Any Power in any satanic basket, enslaving the souls of men in this country/city, you shall not locate my household, die, in the name of Jesus.
3. Powers that have seized the glory of this country / city, over my life, die, in the name of Jesus.
4. Powers collecting the blessings of the resident of this country/city, I and my family are not your candidate, die, in the name of Jesus.

5. Satanic basket, abhorring my blessings in this country/ city, catch fire and burn in to ashes, in the name of Jesus.

6. I release myself from the bondage of any satanic basket in this city, in the name of Jesus.

7. Agents of the power in the basket of this country / city, loose your power and die, in the name of Jesus.

8. Any power in the basket, suspended between the heaven and earth, blocking the heaven over this country / city for my sake, die, in the name of Jesus.

9. Problems in this country / city, emanating from any evil basket, die, in the name of Jesus.

10. Satanic power in a basket, that swallow's virtues of the resident of this country/city, vomit my virtues and die, in the name of Jesus.

11. Satanic goddess in a basket, controlling the lives of the people in this country/city, my life is not your candidate, die, in the name of Jesus.

12. O Lord, I am tired fight my battles, fight for me, in the name of Jesus.

13. Satanic collector of destiny in this city, die, in the name of Jesus.

14. Powers in this city, that reduce great men to nothing, loose your hold over my life and die, in the name of Jesus.

15. I and my household refuse to labor under any bondage of the powers of darkness in this country/city, in the name of Jesus.

16. You this country/city, you shall enlarge me and my entire household and destroy our enemies, in the name of Jesus.
17. Thank you, Lord, for answered prayers, in the name of Jesus.

The Lord Shall Perfect All that Concerneth Me

Bible Reading and Confession

The Lord will perfect that which concerneth me: thy mercy, O Lord, endureth forever: forsake not the works of thine own hands. (Psalm 138:8)

Praise and Worship

Prayer Points

1. I receive the spirit of perfection in my life, marriage, business and career, in the name of Jesus.
2. O Lord, arise and perfect all that concerneth me, in the name of Jesus.
3. I refuse to be a stumbling block to my breakthrough and that of others, in the name of Jesus.
4. I receive the spirit of excellence today, to be above only, in the name of Jesus.
5. I decree, by the power in the blood of Jesus, from today, I shall be highly favored of God, in the name of Jesus.
6. O God of perfection, walk back every second of my life, and correct all my past mistakes, in the name of Jesus.
7. Powers closing the doors of my opportunities before my arrival, die, in the name of Jesus.
8. Powers making me to lose my divine opportunities, you have failed, die, in the name of Jesus.

9. Spirit of procrastination, attacking me at the edge of breakthrough, die, in the name of Jesus.

10. I command the spirit of perfection of God, begin to work in me, in the name of Jesus.

11. I come out of the domain of failure, to the arena of success, in the name of Jesus.

12. Powers making my helpers walk away from me, enough is enough, die, in the name of Jesus.

13. Powers that are turning great dreams to nothing, I am not your candidate, die, in the name of Jesus.

14. Powers that abort great dreams at infancy, over my dreams, I render you impotent, die, in the name of Jesus.

15. I command, the anointing that made Jesus to be successful in his ministry on earth to fall on me, and make me successful in my divine appointment, in the name of Jesus.

16. O Lord, open the door of mercy unto me today, in the name of Jesus.

17. Thank you, Lord, for answered prayers, in the name of Jesus.

Bible Reading and Confession

An ungodly man diggeth up evil: and in his lips there is as a burning fire.
(Proverbs 16:27)

He that diggeth a pit shall fall into it; and whoso breaketh an hedge, a serpent shall bite him. (Ecclesiastes 10:8)

Whoso diggeth a pit shall fall therein: and he that rolleth a stone, it will return upon him. (Proverbs 26:27)

Praise and Worship

Prayer Points

1. I decree, the evil trap of the wicked shall not catch me, in the name of Jesus.
2. Every enemy of my glory, be exposed by fire, in the name of Jesus.
3. I command owner of evil load in my life, carry your load, in the name of Jesus.
4. Any satanic agent, introducing evil into my life at the hours of the night, die, in the name of Jesus.
5. Any satanic agent, introducing sickness into my life at the hours of the night, die, in the name of Jesus.
6. Any satanic power, within my environment introducing poverty into my life, at the hours of the night, die, in the name of Jesus.

7. Powers in-charge of my problems, in the place that I live, die, in the name of Jesus.

8. Any power of the terminator, assigned to terminate me before my time, you are a liar, die, in the name of Jesus.

9. Any satanic curse, making good things to disappear from life, die, in the name of Jesus.

10. You the ground of _____ (Mention the country you are living) you shall not eat my flesh or drink my blood, in the name of Jesus.

11. Every evil pit dug for my sake, be filled with the blood of Jesus, in the name of Jesus.

12. O Lord, make my enemies to eat their own flesh and drink their own blood, in the name of Jesus.

13. Any pit dug for my destiny, swallow your digger, in the name of Jesus.

14. I withdraw my name and that of my children from the grave of untimely death, in the name of Jesus.

15. My name, become too hot for the enemy to call, in the name of Jesus.

16. Any power calling my name for evil at the hours of the night, choke and die, in the name of Jesus.

17. Every evil plan of household wickedness for my life in this year, go back to the planner, in the name of Jesus.

18. I receive power from the throne of grace, to rise above every evil plan of the enemy for my life, in the name of Jesus.

19. I decree and declare, he that wants my home to be empty, shall go empty, in the name of Jesus.

20. Thank Lord, for the answered prayers, in the name of Jesus.

Prayers for Open Doors

Bible Reading and Confession

I know thy works: behold, I have set before thee an open door, and no man can shut it: for thou hast a little strength, and hast kept my word, and hast not denied my name. (Revelation 3:8)

For a great door and effectual is opened unto me, and there are many adversaries. (1 Corinthians 16:9)

Praise and Worship

Prayer Points

1. Begin to thank God for the key of David, that opens any door, in the name of Jesus.
2. Begin to thank God for the power of open doors, in the name of Jesus.
3. Every power that is against my open doors in this country/city, die, in the name of Jesus.
4. Any power that is saying no, to my success in this land country/city, die, in the name of Jesus.
5. Any satanic obstacle standing between me and my open doors, be destroyed by the earth quake of God, in the name of Jesus.
6. O Lord, open unto me doors of breakthroughs now, in the name of Jesus.
7. O Lord, open unto me doors of great success, in the name of Jesus.
8. O Lord, open unto me doors of great opportunities in this country/city, in the name of Jesus.

9. O Lord, open unto me doors of dumbfounding promotion, in the name of Jesus.

10. O Lord, open unto me doors of great testimonies in this country/city, in the name of Jesus.

11. Lord Jesus, cause me to laugh again in this country/city, in the name of Jesus.

12. I receive power to enter my open doors, in the name of Jesus.

13. Lord Jesus, catapult me into greatness by your strong arm, in the name of Jesus.

14. In this year, I receive power to prosper, in the name of Jesus.

15. Every witchcraft projection for me this year, be nullified, in the name of Jesus.

16. I decree and declare this year, I shall not be hidden, in the name of Jesus.

17. I declare this year, as my year of blessing, in the name of Jesus.

18. In this year, I command all my divine helpers, to receive the power to see and locate me by fire, in the name of Jesus.

19. Foundational yoke closing great doors against me, break, in the name of Jesus.

20. Father Lord, I thank you, for answered prayers, in the name of Jesus.

Bible Reading and Confession

And the Lord shall make thee the head, and not the tail; and thou shalt be above only, and thou shalt not be beneath; if that thou hearken unto the commandments of the Lord thy God, which I command thee this day, to observe and to do them: (Deuteronomy 28:13)

Praise and Worship

Prayer Points

1. I refuse my angel of blessing to depart, in the name of Jesus.
2. I paralyze all aggression address to my star, in the name of Jesus.
3. Let God arise in his anger and fight my war for me, in the name of Jesus.
4. O Lord, bring honey out of the rock for me, in the name of Jesus.
5. O Lord, open the good doors of life that household wickedness has shut, in the name of Jesus.
6. Let anti-breakthrough design against my life, be shattered to irreparable pieces, in the name of Jesus.
7. O Lord, uproot from my life evil plantation that are against my advancement, in the name of Jesus.
8. O Lord, plant into my life good things that will advance my life, in the name of Jesus.

9. Let every anti-progress altars erected against me, be destroyed with the fire of God, in the name of Jesus.

10. I paralyze all spiritual wolves working against my life, in the name of Jesus.

11. I withdraw my benefits from the hands of the oppressors, in the name of Jesus.

12. Let every power chasing away my blessings, be paralyzed, in the name of Jesus.

13. Let every spiritual weakness in my life receive permanent termination, in the name of Jesus.

14. I render null and void, the effect of any interaction with satanic agents that are moving around as men and women, in the name of Jesus.

15. Every imprisoned and buried potentials, come forth now by fire, in the name of Jesus.

16. Let the anointing to excel and the power to prosper, fall mightily upon my life, in the name of Jesus.

17. Father Lord, I thank you for answered prayers, in the name of Jesus.

Prayer for Wealth Transfer

Bible Reading and Confession: 2 Kings 7

I sent you to reap that whereon ye bestowed no labour: other men laboured, and ye are entered into their labours." (John 4:38)

Praise and Worship

Prayer Points

1. I will not squander my divine opportunities, in the name of Jesus.
2. I refuse to be a wandering star, in the name of Jesus.
3. Let the riches of the gentiles be transferred to me, in the name of Jesus.
4. Any power causing wealth failure in my life, die, in the name of Jesus.
5. Lord Jesus, touch my purse and fill it with your divine wealth, in the name of Jesus.
6. By the wealthy name of Jesus, let the heavenly resources rush to my door post, in the name of Jesus.
7. I bind every spirit of debt, for I shall not borrow to eat, in the name of Jesus.
8. I recover all my blessings in any body of water, forest and satanic bank, in the name of Jesus.
9. O Lord, disappoint the devices of the enemies fashioned against my finances, in the name of Jesus.
10. O Lord, create a new and profitable opportunities for me, in the name of Jesus.

11. I bind the spirit of fake and useless investments, in the name of Jesus.
12. I break the control of the spirit of poverty over my life, in the name of Jesus.
13. I will rise above all the unbeliever around me, in the name of Jesus.
14. Every curse pronounced against my source of income, break, in the name of Jesus.
15. Every effect of cursed house and land upon my prosperity, break, in the name of Jesus.
16. O Lord, plug my life into your divine prosperity, in the name of Jesus.
17. Every familiar spirit sharing my money, before I receive it, be bound permanently, in the name of Jesus.
18. Let the anointing of excellence fall on me, in the name of Jesus.
19. I remove my name from the book of financial embarrassment, in the name of Jesus.
20. I decree, the riches of the gentiles shall be my possession, in the name of Jesus.
21. I command divine magnet of prosperity, to be planted in my hands, in the name of Jesus.
22. Wealth locate me by fire, in the name of Jesus.
23. I speak destruction unto the spirit of poverty in my life, in the name of Jesus.
24. Father Lord, I thank you for answered prayers, in the name of Jesus.

Bible Reading and Confession: 1 Samuel 1:1–28

Wait on the Lord: be of good courage, and he shall strengthen thine heart: wait, I say, on the Lord. (Psalm 27:14)

Praise and Worship

Prayer Points

1. I release myself from the bondage of any evil altar, in the name of Jesus.
2. I vomit every satanic poison that I have swallowed, in the name of Jesus.
3. I curse every local altar fashioned against me, in the name of Jesus.
4. Anything done against my life with demonic anointing, be nullified, in the name of Jesus.
5. Every decision, vow or promises made by my fore father's contrary to my divine destiny, lose your hold by fire, in the name of Jesus.
6. Every legal ground that ancestral / guardian spirit has over my life, be destroyed, in the name of Jesus.
7. Every hold of any sacrifice ever offered in my father's house, or on my behalf, I break your powers, in the name of Jesus.
8. I decree in the name of Jesus, the height nobody has ever attain in my family and generation, I will attain in life, in the name of Jesus.

9. Any power prolonging my journey to breakthrough, fall down and die, in the name of Jesus.

10. I break every covenants and curses of the spirit of the snail in my life, in the name of Jesus.

11. Every evil effect of the spirit of the snail over my life, be destroyed, in the name of Jesus.

12. Any spirit chasing away my blessings, be destroyed, in the name of Jesus.

13. O Lord, I reject left over blessing, I claim my original, in the name of Jesus.

14. I reject the spirit of fear, anxiety and discouragement, in the name of Jesus.

15. Every arrow of backwardness fired into my star, die, in the name of Jesus.

16. Every arrow of evil delay fired into my life, die, in the name of Jesus.

17. Any satanic chain of stagnation in any department of my life, break, in the name of Jesus.

18. Any satanic arrow of shame and disgrace, targeted at my life, backfire, in the name of Jesus.

19. Any power ordained to make me rise and fall, die, in the name of Jesus.

20. Curses and covenants of satanic delay, break, in the name of Jesus.

21. Cloud of darkness around my breakthroughs, scatter, in the name of Jesus.

22. I pull down every stronghold of satanic delay, in the name of Jesus.

23. Chains of delay holding down my star, break, in the name of Jesus.

24. Any power of my father's house, delaying my breakthrough, die, in the name of Jesus.

25. Deep pit swallowing my virtues, vomit them by fire, in the name of Jesus.
26. My glory, wherever you are, arise, sit up and begin to speak, in the name of Jesus.
27. Father Lord, I thank you for answered prayers, in the name of Jesus.

Bible Reading and Confession

And say, Thus saith the Lord God; Woe to the women that sew pillows to all armholes, and make kerchiefs upon the head of every stature to hunt souls! Will ye hunt the souls of my people, and will ye save the souls alive that come unto you? And will ye pollute me among my people for handfuls of barley and for pieces of bread, to slay the souls that should not die, and to save the souls alive that should not live, by your lying to my people that hear your lies? Wherefore thus saith the Lord God; Behold, I am against your pillows, wherewith ye there hunt the souls to make them fly, and I will tear them from your arms, and will let the souls go, even the souls that ye hunt to make them fly. Your kerchiefs also will I tear, and deliver my people out of your hand, and they shall be no more in your hand to be hunted; and ye shall know that I am the Lord. (Ezekiel 13:18–21)

Praise and Worship

Prayer Points

1. Every evil conspiracy in the second heaven, on earth, underneath the earth, or in the waters against this ministry, be scattered, in the name of Jesus.
2. You evil strongman in charge of this state, somersault and die, in the name of Jesus.

3. Every satanic agent spying on this ministry and reporting to the enemies, be exposed and be disgraced, in the name of Jesus.

4. It is written "The enemies shall be afraid out of their hiding places", therefore you enemies of progress of this ministry, let fear and panic grip your minds, in the name of Jesus.

5. O Lord, tear down every evil altar and charms used to ensnare the members of this ministry, in the name of Jesus.

6. All evil mountains in this state, against this ministry, fall down and die, in the name of Jesus.

7. O Lord, by your power which no man can defy, open the doors of miracles and wonders in this ministry, in the name of Jesus.

8. Any power hunting for the glory of this ministry, fall down and die, in the name of Jesus.

9. Any power hunting for the soul of the members of this ministry, fall down and die, in the name of Jesus.

10. Woe unto that power that sow evil band against this ministry, in the name of Jesus.

11. Any satanic agent making evil veil for the men and women of this ministry, your time is up, die, in the name of Jesus.

12. Any power sewing evil veil to cover the glory of this ministry, fall down and die, in the name of Jesus.

13. Any power lying to divert men and women away from this ministry, you shall not succeed, die, in the name of Jesus.

14. Any magic band sow against this ministry, catch fire and burn to ashes, in the name of Jesus.

15. Every evil veil covering the faces of people in this ministry, catch fire and burn to ashes, in the name of Jesus.
16. Father Lord, I thank you for answered prayers, in the name of Jesus.

My Head shall be Lifted Up

Bible Reading and Confession

And now shall mine head be lifted up above mine enemies round about me: therefore, will I offer in his tabernacle sacrifices of joy; I will sing, yea, I will sing praises unto the Lord. (Psalm 27:6)

Praise and Worship

Prayer Points

1. Let every demonic trap set against my life be shattered to pieces, in the name of Jesus.
2. You my head, refuse to cooperate with the enemy, in the name of Jesus.
3. O Lord, send your fire to the foundation of my life and uproot every evil foundational power working against my destiny, in the name of Jesus.
4. I release myself from the bondage of evil attachments, in the name of Jesus.
5. I paralyze all evil powers delaying my miracles, in the name of Jesus.
6. Let the agents of impossibility working against my desired miracles, be completely paralyzed, in the name of Jesus.
7. Holy Ghost fire, let the good things buried in my life, begin to come alive now, in the name of Jesus.
8. O Lord, hide me in your secret place, away from the arrows of the wicked, in the name of Jesus.

9. O Lord, let my enemies be drunken with their blood and let those that seek my life eat their own flesh, in the name of Jesus.

10. Father Lord, lift me high above my enemies round about me, in the name of Jesus.

11. Every arrow of problem fired into my life, go back to your sender, in the name of Jesus.

12. O Lord, let the evil projection of my enemies become their lot in this year, in the name of Jesus.

13. Lord Jesus, shine your face upon me, in the name of Jesus.

14. Lord Jesus, fight my battle for me in the name of Jesus.

15. I command every evil altar erected against me to become the burial place of all my enemies, in Jesus name

16. Any demoting power over my life, die, in the name of Jesus.

17. My head reject bewitchment, in the name of Jesus.

18. Any satanic incantation reigned against my head, die, in the name of Jesus.

19. Any power calling my head for evil, die, in the name of Jesus.

20. My head come alive by fire, in the name of Jesus.

21. Satan, loose your hold over my life, in the name of Jesus.

22. Whether the devil likes it or not, my head shall be a crown of glory, in the name of Jesus.

23. Father Lord, I thank you for answered prayers, in the name of Jesus.

I Shall not be Barren in a Fertile Land

Bible Reading and Confession

And the tree of the field shall yield her fruit, and the earth shall yield her increase, and they shall be safe in their land, and shall know that I am the Lord, when I have broken the bands of their yoke, and delivered them out of the hand of those that served themselves of them. (Ezekiel 34:27)

Then shall the earth yield her increase; and God, even our own God, shall bless us. (Psalm 67:6)

Then I will give you rain in due season, and the land shall yield her increase, and the trees of the field shall yield their fruit. (Leviticus 26:4)

Praise and Worship

Prayer Points

1. O Lord, I shall make it in the land of the living, in the name of Jesus.
2. O Lord, cause my whole heart to be at rest, trusting in you, in the name of Jesus.
3. Let the blood of Jesus poison the roots of all my problems, in the name of Jesus.
4. I tear down the stronghold of Satan against my ground, in the name of Jesus.
5. Satan, I command you to leave my land with all your demons, in the name of Jesus.

6. O Lord, you shall make a way for me where there's no way, in the name of Jesus.

7. O Lord, I shall be fruitful in your vineyard, in the name of Jesus.

8. O Lord, let the land and all that is in it, yield increase unto me, in the name of Jesus.

9. I shall not be barren in this land, in the name of Jesus.

10. You the spirit of hard labor without fruit in my life, die, in the name of Jesus.

11. Every spirit of famine in my life, die, in the name of Jesus.

12. Lord Jesus, increase me with your power, in the name of Jesus.

13. This land, yield your harvest to me now, in the name of Jesus.

14. Lord Jesus, give me what is good in this season, in the name of Jesus.

15. O God, my father, bless me greatly in this month, in the name of Jesus.

16. Father Lord, I thank you for answered prayers, in the name of Jesus.

I Defeat Every Contrary Handwriting Against my Destiny

Bible Reading and Confession:

Blotting out the handwriting of ordinances that was against us, which was contrary to us, and took it out of the way, nailing it to his cross; And having spoiled principalities and powers, he made a shew of them openly, triumphing over them in it. (Colossians 2:14–15)

Praise and Worship

Prayer Points

1. I refuse to harbor any prayer killer in every department of my life, in the name of Jesus.
2. I remove every demonic signature against my destiny, in the name of Jesus.
3. I nullify every contrary handwriting against my destiny, in the name of Jesus.
4. Every anti-excellence spirit, lose your hold upon my life, in the name of Jesus.
5. I dismantle every demonic opposition to my breakthroughs, in the name of Jesus.
6. Every satanic case file against my life be closed, by the blood of Jesus.
7. I overthrow every demonic judgement directed against my destiny, in the name of Jesus.
8. I defeat every handwriting of the devil against my marriage, in Jesus name.

9. I defeat every handwriting of evil against my children, in the name of Jesus.

10. I defeat every satanic handwriting against my star, in Jesus name.

11. I defeat every handwriting of evil covenant over my career, in Jesus name.

12. I defeat every handwriting of miscarriage of good things in my life, in the mighty name of Jesus.

13. Every satanic handwriting of poverty, standing at the door of my breakthrough, be cancelled, by the blood of Jesus.

14. Let the handwriting of the Lord, overtake every satanic handwriting in my life, in Jesus name.

15. O Lord, disgrace every satanic handwriting in my life today, in the name of Jesus.

16. Father Lord, I thank you for answered prayers, in the name of Jesus.

I Shall Pursue, Overtake and Recover All

Bible Reading and Confession

And David enquired at the Lord, saying, Shall I pursue after this troop? shall I overtake them? And he answered him, pursue: for thou shalt surely overtake them, and without fail recover all. (1Samuel 30:8)

Praise and Worship

Prayer Points

1. I stand against every satanic operation, hindering my blessings, in the name of Jesus.
2. Every wicked spirit planning to rob me of the will of God, fall down and die, in the name of Jesus.
3. I confound every stubborn pursuer, in the name of Jesus.
4. Every witchcraft power, stealing my blessing, I cast you into outer darkness, in the name of Jesus.
5. Angels of the Living God, arise, pursue, overtake, and recover all my stolen blessings, in the name of Jesus.
6. I shall not labor for my enemies, in the name of Jesus.
7. Holy Ghost, arise and restore all my stolen blessings, in million folds, in the name of Jesus.
8. I bind any strong man or strong woman, in possession of my goods, and I take back my goods, in the name of Jesus.
9. Any power that has stolen from my life, restore back to me today all you have stolen, in the name of Jesus.

10. Any power impersonating me at the hours of the night, collecting what belongs to me, die, in the name of Jesus.

11. I collect back my possessions from the hands of my oppressors, in Jesus name.

12. You family familiar spirit, standing against my advancement, die today by fire, in the name of Jesus.

13. In the name of Jesus, I walk my way back to my throne, in the name of Jesus.

14. I shall not serve my enemies, in the name of Jesus.

15. O Lord, thank you for answered prayers, in the name Jesus.

The Lord Shall Lift up a Standard against my Enemies

Bible Reading and Confession

So shall they fear the name of the Lord from the west, and his glory from the rising of the sun. When the enemy shall come in like a flood, the Spirit of the Lord shall lift up a standard against him. (Isaiah 59:19)

Praise and Worship

Prayer Points

1. O Lord, let the enemies fall by their own counsels, in the name of Jesus.
2. Arise O Lord, in your anger and lift up yourself, because of the rage of my enemies, in the name of Jesus.
3. O Lord, let the enemies of my soul, fall into pit dug for me, in Jesus name.
4. O Lord, let all my enemies be ashamed and be troubled, in Jesus name.
5. O Lord, fight against them that fight against me, in the name of Jesus.
6. Let the way of my enemies, be dark and slippery, in the name of Jesus.
7. O Lord, let the sorrows of my enemies be multiplied, in the name of Jesus.
8. O Lord, restore me to your original plan for my life, in Jesus name.

9. Lord Jesus, let any power that undertake any deep sleep in order to harm me, die suddenly, in Jesus name.

10. Lord Jesus, let the home of the wicked against me become desolate by fire, in the name of Jesus.

11. O Lord, let your angels of destruction, locate the camp of every enemy pretending to be my friend, in the name of Jesus.

12. Lord Jesus, sweep my problems away with your broom of destruction, in Jesus name.

13. Every Achan in the camp of my life, receive the stones of fire, in Jesus name.

14. Every Judas selling me out, be eaten up by divine worms, in Jesus name.

15. O Lord, raise a mighty standard against the powers that has risen up against my life, in the name of Jesus.

16. O Lord, thank you for answered prayers, in the name of Jesus.

Bible Reading and Confession

And he will be a wild man; his hand will be against every man, and every man's hand against him; and he shall dwell in the presence of all his brethren.
(Genesis 16:12)

Praise and Worship

Prayer Points

1. Ishmael of my father's house, enough is enough, loose me and let me go, in the name of Jesus.
2. Ishmael of my mother's house, enough is enough, I break off your chain of slavery in my life, in Jesus name.
3. I refuse to be a slave to any Ishmael, in the name of Jesus.
4. Ishmael hear the word of the living God, you shall not overcome me, in the name of Jesus.
5. Ishmael at my place of work, ministering on any evil altar against me, receive the Hammer of God, in the name of Jesus.
6. I break myself loose from any collective captivity, of the powers of Ishmael in my family, in the name of Jesus.
7. My Ishmael shall die today, in the name of Jesus.
8. O God of Elijah, put my Ishmael in an everlasting bondage, in Jesus name.

9. Every power of Ishmael seeking to destroy my God given destiny, die, in the name of Jesus.

10. I receive my freedom from the demonic power, that controls my father's house, in the name of Jesus.

11. Any power shouting to shut down my destiny, be silenced forever, in Jesus name.

12. I move from the valley to the mountain top, in the name of Jesus.

13. Ishmael of my marriage, your time is up, die, in the name of Jesus.

14. Every satanic barrier standing between me and my breakthrough, break and scatter, in the name of Jesus.

15. Angels of the Lord, guide me to the top by the sword of fire, in the name of Jesus.

16. O Lord, I thank you for answered prayers, in the name of Jesus.

Bible Reading and Confession
Genesis 19

Praise and Worship

Prayer Points

1. Every spirit of Sodom and Gomorrah in my life, die, in the name of Jesus.
2. Every spirit of self-destruction forcing me into error, die, in the name of Jesus.
3. I refuse to listen to any demonic voice that wants to destroy me, in the name of Jesus.
4. You anti-Christ spirit in this world, you will not locate my household, in the name of Jesus.
5. Spirit of lust, die in my life, in the name of Jesus.
6. Every spirit of disobedience to God's word in my life, die, in Jesus name.
7. I refuse to be God's enemy, in the name of Jesus.
8. Lord Jesus, renew your spirit within me, in Jesus name.
9. I refuse to walk after the flesh, in the name of Jesus.
10. Lord Jesus, let the spirit of holiness possess me, in Jesus name.
11. O Lord, counter every attempt of the devil to sway me from your presence, in Jesus name.
12. My heart, become the habitation of the Holy Ghost, in the name of Jesus.
13. The light of my salvation shall not grow dark, in the name of Jesus.

14. I receive power to overcome the flesh in my life, in the name of Jesus.
15. Sing this song 7 times "If I be a child of God, let fire fall"
16. Fire of God, incubate my life, in the name of Jesus.
17. O Lord, I thank you for answered prayers, in the name of Jesus.

My Haman Shall Die

Bible Reading and Confession
Esther 3

Praise and Worship

Prayer Points

1. Haman of my existence, what are you waiting for? Die, in the name of Jesus.
2. O Lord, let the counsel and the evil plot of my Haman become his lot, in the name of Jesus.
3. Haman of my happiness, die, in the name of Jesus.
4. Haman of my glory, die, in the name of Jesus.
5. O Lord, use my Haman to announce me, in the name of Jesus.
6. Consciously or unconsciously, my Haman shall speak for my favor, in the name of Jesus.
7. Any power that says, over their dead body will I be a testimony in this life, what are you waiting for? Die, in the name of Jesus.
8. Any evil pit dug for me, my Haman shall fall there in, in Jesus name.
9. Every Haman plotting my death, die in my place, in the name of Jesus.
10. Every wicked conspiracy of the enemy against me, be converted for my favor and cause my promotion, in Jesus name.
11. Every Haman around me, I paralyze your activities, in the name of Jesus.

12. O Lord, trouble the sleep of those troubling my life, in the name of Jesus.

13. Jehovah Sabaoth, manifest in the dream of my Haman, as the mighty terrible God, in the name of Jesus.

14. O Lord, your word says, "The word which you have spoken shall not return to you void". Father, let your promises be fulfilled in my life now, in the name of Jesus.

15. I receive the divine mandate for peace, joy, prosperity, and happiness in my life, in the name of Jesus.

16. O Lord, I thank you for answered prayers, in the name of Jesus.

I Take Back My Generational Well of Blessing

Bible Reading and Confession
Genesis 26

Praise and Worship

Prayer Points

1. Every generational blessing dated back to the time of my forefathers, I collect them today, in the name of Jesus.

2. Any power claiming ownership over my generational blessing, die, in the name of Jesus.

3. Any power that is stopping the flow of my generational blessing, die, in the name of Jesus.

4. Every satanic blocker of good things in my life, die, in the name of Jesus.

5. I command the well of my blessings to begin to spring forth, in Jesus name.

6. Lord Jesus, help me to locate all my family forgotten wealth in the hand of the enemy and bring them to me, in the name of Jesus.

7. Any power contending with me over my generational wealth, die, in the name of Jesus.

8. Let the covenant of divine wealth for my family come alive in me, in Jesus name.

9. I receive power to take over my possession that the enemies seized all these years, in the name of Jesus.

10. O God of Rehoboth, give me peace now from all my struggles, in Jesus name.

11. Lord Jesus, move me from the position of not enough to abundance, in the name of Jesus.

12. Every spirit of fruitless hard work, die, in the name of Jesus.

13. The word of God says "I shall be the head and not the tail". Today, I claim the anointing of the head, in the name of Jesus.

14. O Lord, give me my portion of wealth in this land, as you did for Abraham, in the name of Jesus.

15. O Lord, make me a pillar of my father's house, in the name of Jesus.

16. Father Lord, I thank you for answered prayers, in the name of Jesus.

O Lord, Let your Will for My Life come Forth by Fire

Bible Reading and Confession

And Adam said, This is now bone of my bones, and flesh of my flesh: she shall be called Woman, because she was taken out of Man. (Genesis 2:23)

And Adam called his wife's name Eve; because she was the mother of all living. (Genesis 3:20)

Praise and Worship

Prayer Points

1. Lord, bring forth the man/woman you created for me, in the name of Jesus.
2. I reject any satanic man/woman projected for me, in the name of Jesus.
3. Any power behind marital delay in my life, fall down and die, in the name of Jesus.
4. I erase from my body any mark of rejection placed upon me to delay my marriage, in the name of Jesus.
5. Any power within and around me chasing away the will of God for my life, die, in the name of Jesus.
6. I refuse to remain on the shelf of marital delay, in the name of Jesus.
7. Every covenant of marital delay in my life, break, in the name of Jesus.

8. Powers preventing me from getting married, enough is enough, release me and die, in the name of Jesus.

9. Any satanic veil covering my face, preventing me to be seen, be roasted, by fire, in the name of Jesus.

10. O Lord, make my marriage come to pass this year, in the name of Jesus.

11. Any satanic barrier standing between me and my husband/wife, be consumed by fire, in the name of Jesus.

12. I claim back my marital life by fire, in the name of Jesus.

13. Spirit of marital delay, you have no right over me, die, in the name of Jesus.

14. Any power claiming ownership over me, preventing my earthly marriage, die, in the name of Jesus.

15. Any spirit husband/wife existing, preventing me from getting married physically, fall down and die, in the name of Jesus.

16. O Lord, bring my husband/wife to me, in the name of Jesus.

17. I shall not die a spinster/bachelor, in the name of Jesus.

18. Any power that has use my life to make a demonic vow, die, with your vow, in the name of Jesus.

19. Lord Jesus, send your ministering angles to bring forth my husband/wife to me, in the name of Jesus.

20. Powers of my father's house and my mother's house behind this problem in my life, your time is up, die, in the name of Jesus.

21. O Lord, let your name be glorified as I get married in this year, in the name of Jesus.

22. Lord Jesus, I thank you for answered prayers, in Jesus name.

Bible Reading / Confession:

So we boiled my son, and did eat him: and I said unto her on the next day,
Give thy son, that we may eat him: and she hath hid her son. (2Kings 6:29)

Behold, I have created the smith that bloweth the coals in the fire, and that bringeth forth an instrument for his work; and I have created the waster to destroy. (Isaiah 54:16)

Praise and Worship

Prayer Points

1. Any power on assignment to waste me, be wasted, in the name of Jesus.
2. Wasters of destiny of my father's house, my destiny is not your lot, die, in the name of Jesus.
3. Wasters of destiny of my mother's house, my destiny is not your lot, die, in the name of Jesus.
4. My children and I are not for the wasters of this generation, in the name of Jesus.
5. I shall not be wasted, in the name of Jesus.
6. I refuse to become a sacrifice of promotion for satanic wasters, in the name of Jesus.
7. I decree and declare, my story shall not be, he came into this world and left without achieving great things, in the name of Jesus.

8. Any power, pronouncing death upon my destiny, die, in the name of Jesus.

9. Every waster of life in my territory, the Lord rebuke you, die, in the name of Jesus.

10. I declare and decree, my children shall not be wasted by wasters of this generation, in the name of Jesus.

11. Whether the devil likes it or not, I shall fulfill my destiny, in the name of Jesus.

12. I shall not die before my time, in the name of Jesus.

13. Every instrument of the wasters, set in motion against me and my household, die, in the name of Jesus.

14. Local forces reducing lives to nothing in this area, my life is not your candidate, die, in the name of Jesus.

15. Any power using my life to negotiate for promotion, die, in the name of Jesus.

16. Any power using my life to negotiate for wealth, die, in the name of Jesus.

17. Any power that is not happy because I am alive, die, in the name of Jesus.

18. My father, my father, arrest all evil wasters on assignment against me, in the name of Jesus.

19. Any power using the sun, moon and the stars to fight against my destiny, die, in the name of Jesus.

20. I move out of the prison of non-achievement, to the realm of fulfillment, in the name of Jesus.

21. Wasters in the camp of my life, be wasted, in the name of Jesus.

22. I release the tornado of the almighty God, against any evil plantation that is against my destiny, in the name of Jesus

23. Power of God, lift me above every satanic strategy of the wasters over my life, in the name of Jesus.

24. By the power of the most high God, I waste the devices of the wasters fashioned against my children, in the name of Jesus.

25. Power of God, lift me above every satanic arrow fired at me, in the name of Jesus.

26. I receive power to laugh my enemies to scorn, in the name of Jesus.

27. O Lord, show yourself mighty and strong in my life, against the powers of the wasters operating around me, in the name of Jesus.

28. Lord Jesus, I thank you for the answered prayer.

My Eagle shall Fly

Bible Reading and Confession

But they that wait upon the Lord shall renew their strength; they shall mount up with wings as eagles; they shall run, and not be weary; and they shall walk, and not faint. (Isaiah 40:31)

Who satisfies your years with good things, So that your youth is renewed like the eagle. (Psalm 103:5)

Praise and Worship

Prayer Points

1. My eagle, hear the word of the living God, you shall not dwell with the chickens of this world, in the name of Jesus.
2. My eagle, I command you to take your rightful position, in the name of Jesus.
3. Powers pulling my eagle down, die, in the name of Jesus
4. My eagle, receive the divine power of God and soar high in life, in the name of Jesus.
5. Any power caging my eagle, die, in the name of Jesus.
6. I receive power to soar higher in life than my contemporaries, in the name of Jesus.
7. Powers of satanic limitation in any department of my life, die, in the name of Jesus.
8. Seeds of greatness in me begin to spring forth from today, in the name of Jesus.

9. Any power that placed a dormant decree on my life, die, in the name of Jesus.

10. I shall fly high, I shall not be reduced to nothing in life, in the name of Jesus.

11. Every evil decree of my father's house limiting my potentials, die, in the name of Jesus.

12. Ancient gate of darkness locked against my advancement in life, open by fire and let me go, in the name of Jesus.

13. Every evil decree of my mother's house limiting my potentials, die, in the name of Jesus.

14. I receive divine assistance from above, to be above only and not beneath, in the name of Jesus.

15. In every department of life, I shall be the head, in the name of Jesus.

16. O Lord, command everything you created and you used man to create to begin to work for my favor from today, in the name of Jesus.

17. I take back my position among the eagle, created by God, in the name of Jesus.

18. I shall rule and not be ruled over by the chickens of this world, in Jesus name.

19. Any power assigned to dethrone me from the throne of my destiny, receive the stone of fire, in the name of Jesus.

20. By Fire and by force, I wake up from my physical and spiritual slumber, in the name of Jesus.

21. I reactivate every divine covenant of champion that is dormant in my life, in the name of Jesus.

22. Holy Ghost fire, pursue the enemies of my divine position, in the name of Jesus.

23. Every river Jordan standing between me and my promised land, dry up by fire, in the name of Jesus.

24. Every satanic idol crying against my life, be silenced forever, in the name of Jesus.

25. Any problem I inherited from my parent, that is scattering my dreams, die, in the name of Jesus.

26. Lord Jesus, I thank you for answered prayers, in Jesus name.

The Evil Vow of the Enemy, Shall Destroy the Enemy

Bible Reading and Confession: Acts 23:12–21

Associate yourselves, O ye people, and ye shall be broken in pieces; and give ear, all ye of far countries: gird yourselves, and ye shall be broken in pieces; gird yourselves, and ye shall be broken in pieces. (Isaiah 8:9)

Praise and Worship

Prayer Points

1. Every satanic gathering and their vow against me, be destroyed by the fire of God, in the name of Jesus.
2. Every satanic divination against me and my household, fall down to the ground and die, in the name of Jesus.
3. Satanic enterprises shall not be established in my home, in the name of Jesus.
4. Every satanic vow made against my father and mother, that is manifesting in my life, die, in the name of Jesus.
5. Any satanic mouth calling my name for evil at the hours of the night, be silenced forever, in the name of Jesus.
6. Every evil decree issued against my life, shall not stand, in the name of Jesus.
7. Every evil judgement passed against me at the hours of the night, by witchcraft powers, fall down and die, in the name of Jesus.

8. Every evil plan of the enemy to demote me, in any area of life, back fire by fire, in the name of Jesus.

9. I decree satanic vows shall not catch up with my destiny, in the name of Jesus.

10. It is written," Any tree that my father has not planted shall be uprooted" (Matthew 15:13). Therefore, I command right now, you evil growth in my life, be uprooted by fire, in the name of Jesus.

11. I command the ground to open and swallow every evil gathering of the enemy against my life and that of my household, in the name of Jesus.

12. I command the plan of the enemy against me and my household, to cause their death, in the name of Jesus.

13. Let the altar of the enemy erected against my destiny, become their burial place, in the name of Jesus.

14. O Lord, let the evil prayer of the wicked against me become an abomination in your presence, in the name of Jesus.

15. I cancel and nullify any evil prophecy and satanic vow of any demonic prophet cooperating with my enemy against me, in Jesus name.

16. Any problem emanating from demonic incantation of many years, because of my parental involvement, die, in the name of Jesus.

17. I receive power to trample upon every demonic right claimed over my life, by ancestral evil powers, in the name of Jesus.

18. I decree that the plan of the wicked concerning me shall not be my lot, in Jesus name.

19. Holy Ghost fire, consume the enchantment of the wicked against me, in Jesus name.

20. I decree, let the evil gathering of the wicked against me, be scattered, in the name of Jesus.
21. I command every negative word of the enemy spoken against my life, become impotent, in Jesus name.
22. Father Lord, I thank you for the answered prayers, in the name of Jesus.

Prayer for Marital Bliss

Bible Reading and Confession

Whoso findeth a wife findeth a good thing, and obtaineth favour of the Lord. (Proverbs 18:22)

Praise and Worship

Prayer Points

1. Father Lord, I thank you for my spouse, in the name of Jesus.
2. Father Lord, make my home a praise on earth, in the name of Jesus.
3. Any anti-marriage forces from my lineage fighting my marriage, die, in the name of Jesus.
4. O Lord, make my home a tool of salvation, in the name of Jesus.
5. Father Lord, deliver my marriage from the hands of satanic marriage hunters, in the name of Jesus.
6. I decree, no strange man / woman shall locate my husband / wife, in the name of Jesus.
7. Any strange woman /man on assignment to destroy my home, receive angelic slap, in the name of Jesus.
8. O Lord, beautify my home with your unchanging love, in the name of Jesus.
9. My marriage is for signs and wonders, therefore, Satan you have no business in my home, in the name of Jesus.
10. Any power assigned to trouble my spouse, fail woefully, in the name of Jesus.

11. Powers that destroy home in this nation, hear the word of the Lord, you cannot destroy my home, die, in the name of Jesus.

12. Lord Jesus, re-ignite the fire of your love in our home, in the name of Jesus.

13. Spirit of divorce, my marriage is not your candidate, die, in the name of Jesus.

14. O Lord, repair every faulty foundation in my marriage with the blood of Jesus, in the name of Jesus.

15. Every enemy monitoring my marriage for evil, receive blindness, in the name of Jesus.

16. Any power that has vowed, that I will not have a settled home, die, in the name of Jesus.

17. Any satanic spirit that causes failure in marriage, you will not have a place in my home, die, in the name of Jesus.

18. I receive the anointing to be blinded to temptation, in Jesus name.

19. My Marriage is not for sale, in the name of Jesus.

20. I decree my home shall be a place of peace and joy, in the name of Jesus.

21. O Lord, release upon my home the spirit of genuine forgiveness, in the name of Jesus.

22. I decree in this marriage and in this home, fighting, satanic thoughts and evil imagination, shall be found wanting, in the name of Jesus.

23. Powers that make one to be dissatisfy with one's spouse, you will not enter into my life, in the name of Jesus.

24. Robbers of marital bliss, you will not locate my marriage, in the name of Jesus.

25. O Lord, break us down and remold us to fit your purpose in our home, in the name of Jesus.

26. Every satanic adviser with the intention to break my home, run mad by fire, in the name of Jesus.

27. Any stranger outside throwing evil stones against my marriage, roast by fire, in the name of Jesus.

28. I shield my home with the blood of Jesus, in Jesus name.

29. Every good thing that the enemy has destroyed in my marriage, come alive, by the power in the blood of Jesus.

30. I command every foundational problem in my marriage, to be destroyed by fire, in the name of Jesus.

31. Powers from my foundation and my spouse foundation against our union, die, in the name of Jesus.

32. Any evil thing we inherited from our parent, affecting our home, die, in the name of Jesus.

33. The wicked shall not prosper over my home, in the name of Jesus.

34. Father Lord, I thank you for delivering my marriage from the hands of unfriendly friends and satanic agents, in the Jesus name.

My Children Shall be as Olive Tree Around my Table

Bible Reading and Confession

Thy wife shall be as a fruitful vine by the sides of thine house: thy children like olive plants round about thy table. (Psalm 128:3)

Praise and Worship

Prayer Points

1. I decree, my children shall be a source of joy to me, in the name of Jesus.
2. I decree the destiny of my children shall not be perverted, in the name of Jesus.
3. O Lord, help my children to become what you created them to be in life, in the name of Jesus.
4. Evil arrows of my father's house, shall not locate my children, in the name of Jesus.
5. My children, hear the word of the living God, you shall not inherit any evil thing from my life or foundation, in Jesus name.
6. I decree any power that follow me from childhood to destroy my destiny, shall not locate my children, in the name of Jesus.
7. Every satanic covenant of my father's house, my children are not your lot, break, in the name of Jesus.

8. Every Curse of problems and failures at the edge of breakthrough, from my mother's house, my children shall not partake of you, break, in the name of Jesus.

9. Territorial forces around my home that are out to destroy the lives of children, you will not locate my children, die, in the name of Jesus.

10. Spirit of self-destruction in this nation, hear the word of God, my children are not your portion, die, in Jesus name.

11. Arrows of demonic sickness flying around in this country, you will not locate my children, die, in the name of Jesus.

12. Any power running after children in-order to punish the parent, from my place of birth, I render you impotent over my children, in Jesus name.

13. O Lord, baptize my children with the anointing of greatness, excellence and success, in the name of Jesus.

14. Holy Spirit, possess my children from childhood, in the name of Jesus.

15. My children, receive power to do exploit for the Lord in this world, in the name of Jesus.

16. Any satanic power, that divert children to do the wrong things in life, you shall not locate my children, in the name of Jesus.

17. My children shall be the carriers of God's power and fire in their generation, in the name of Jesus.

18. Every activity of household wickedness over the lives of my children, be wasted, in Jesus name.

19. Wasters of glory and time shall not locate my children, in the name of Jesus.

20. This nation, hear the word of the Lord, you shall not be a caldron to my children, in the name of Jesus.

21. O Lord, let the cross of Calvary have its way, in the lives of my children, in the name of Jesus.
22. I will not weep over my children at any point in their lives, in Jesus name.
23. I shall not know the grave of my children, in the name of Jesus.
24. Fire of God, barricade the lives of my children from any evil attack, in the name of Jesus.
25. Lord Jesus, I thank you for answered prayer today, in Jesus name.

I Move in the Speed of Elijah

Bible Reading and Confession

And the hand of the Lord was on Elijah; and he girded up his loins, and ran before Ahab to the entrance of Jezreel. (1Kings 18:46)

Praise and Worship

Prayer Points

1. I receive power to move ahead of my competitors, in Jesus name.
2. Holy Spirit, energize me to move forward, by fire, in Jesus name.
3. Every anointing of slow progress in my life, dry up, in the name of Jesus.
4. Lord Jesus, push me into my breakthrough by fire, in the name of Jesus.
5. I reject the anointing of sluggishness in my life, in the name of Jesus.
6. Spirit of procrastination attacking my progress in life, withered by fire, in the name of Jesus.
7. Whether my enemies like it or not, I shall reach my goal in life, in the name of Jesus.
8. I decree by fire, the sunlight of my glory shall not set at mid-day, in the name of Jesus.
9. I decree, I shall not stop half way to my breakthrough, in Jesus name.

10. Any power that did not allow my parent to seat on the throne of their destiny, lose you hold over my life and die, in Jesus name.

11. I receive the power of God, like in the time of Elijah to beat my enemies and competitors in the race of life, in Jesus name.

12. In the name of Jesus, I command the sun, moon and stars to cooperate with my advancement, in the name of Jesus.

13. Any power hindering my advancement, I clear you away by the fire of the Holy Ghost, in Jesus name.

14. I receive power to mount up with wings as eagle, in the Jesus name.

15. Any satanic gathering awaiting the news of my down fall, be disgraced by fire, in the name of Jesus.

16. I declare by the power in the blood of Jesus, this is my season of Laughter, in the name of Jesus.

17. O Lord, open my mouth over my enemies round about me, in the name of Jesus.

18. I rise above every demonic authority around me, in the name of Jesus.

19. Thou cross of Calvary, take your position in the battle of my life, in the name of Jesus.

20. Every door of blessings shut against me in this land, open by fire, in the name of Jesus.

21. Thou God that bless Abraham in his own time, visit me and make me greater than Abraham, in the name of Jesus.

22. I recover all my lost fertile ground in the possession of the enemy, in the name of Jesus.

23. Thank you, Lord, for answered prayers, in the name of Jesus.

Bible Reading and Confession

Remember ye not the former things, neither consider the things of old.
Behold, I will do a new thing; now it shall spring forth; shall ye not know it? I will even make a way in the wilderness, and rivers in the desert. The beast of the field shall honour me, the dragons and the owls: because I give waters in the wilderness, and rivers in the desert, to give drink to my people, my chosen. (Isaiah 43:18–20)

Therefore if any man be in Christ, he is a new creature: old things are passed away; behold, all things are become new. (2Corinthians 5:17)

And he that sat upon the throne said, Behold, I make all things new. And he said unto me, write: for these words are true and faithful. (Revelation 21:5)

Praise and Worship

Prayer Points

1. I receive power for new beginning in Christ Jesus, in the name of Jesus.
2. Every spirit of error making me to look back, die, in the name of Jesus.
3. I reject the spirit of backwardness, in the name of Jesus.

4. I reject the old Adam in my life, I receive the new Adam, in the name of Jesus.

5. Every evil thing I inherited from my mother's womb, die, in the name of Jesus.

6. Every evil thing I inherited from my father's life, die, in the name of Jesus.

7. I refuse to dwell in my past mistake, O Lord, help me to start afresh now, in the name of Jesus.

8. Any evil power causing distraction in my life, when I am about to make a meaningful decision, your time is up, die, in the name of Jesus.

9. O Lord, I decree from today I shall not hear the voice of the devil, in the name of Jesus.

10. Anything in me that is making me an enemy of God, die, in the name of Jesus.

11. Any wicked power causing me to make mistake, sleep a deep sleep and never wake up again, in Jesus name.

12. God of Elijah, empower me to keep my focus on you, in the name of Jesus.

13. I refuse to live in my past Glory, I move forward by fire in my new Glory, in the name of Jesus.

14. I decree my past shall not destroy my future, in the name of Jesus.

15. O Lord, deposit your power to achieve great things in me, in the name of Jesus.

16. I decree the wicked shall not win any battle over my life, in the name of Jesus.

17. I receive power to trample over every enemy of my new beginning, in the name of Jesus.

18. I break myself loose from any power holding me down to any unpleasant situation in my life, in the name of Jesus.

19. I declare no evil power and plan shall overcome me, in the name of Jesus.

20. I decree, I shall have the last laugh in the battle of life, in the name of Jesus.

21. Any power planning to turn my day to night and my night to day, die, in the name of Jesus.

22. I declare in the name of Jesus, I move from obscurity into lime light, in the name of Jesus.

23. I decree in the name of Jesus, my past shall not kidnap my today and my tomorrow, in Jesus mighty name.

24. Begin to thank the Lord for answered prayers.

Using the Broom of Destruction of the Lord as a Weapon of Warfare

Bible Reading and Confession

I will also make it a possession for the bittern, and pools of water: and I will sweep it with the besom of destruction, saith the Lord of hosts. (Isaiah 14:23)

Praise and Worship

Prayer Points

1. O broom of destruction of the Lord, sweep away my sorrows, in the name of Jesus.
2. Let the broom of destruction of the Lord, sweep away all my problems, in the name of Jesus.
3. I use the broom of destruction of the Lord, as a weapon of destruction against any enemy standing on my way of progress, in the name of Jesus.
4. I use the broom of destruction of the Lord, to sweep back to the sender every evil curse issued against me, in the name of Jesus.
5. I use the broom of destruction of the Lord, to sweep of all anti-progress spirit working against me into the grave, in the name of Jesus.
6. I use the broom of destruction of the Lord, to destroy every evil covenant working against me through the powers of darkness, the name of Jesus.

7. Everything in my life that is not of God, broom of destruction of the Lord, sweep them into the lake of fire, in the name of Jesus.

8. Thou broom of destruction of the Lord, sweep away every sickness in my blood, in the name of Jesus.

9. O Lord, let your broom of destruction locate the head of my stubborn pursuers, in the name of Jesus.

10. Any power that wants me to die, receive the slap of death by the broom of destruction of the Lord, in the name of Jesus.

11. O Lord, let your broom of destruction swing into action against all my enemies and destroy them, in the name of Jesus.

12. Any power working against my joy and testimony, I sweep you into the abyss with the broom of destruction of the lord, in the name of Jesus.

13. Every good thing the enemy have swept out of my life, I sweep back with the broom of the Lord, in the name of Jesus.

14. Spirit of disgrace, I sweep you away from my life with the broom of destruction of the Lord, in the name of Jesus.

15. Spirit of lack, I sweep you away from my life with the broom of destruction of the Lord, in the name of Jesus.

16. Spirit of untimely death, I sweep you away from my life with the broom of destruction of the lord, in the name of Jesus.

17. Terminal diseases, I sweep you away from my life with the broom of destruction of the Lord, in the name of Jesus.

18. Lord Jesus, take your position in the battle of my life, in the name of Jesus.

19. I receive my deliverance by fire from any wicked powers, in the name of Jesus.
20. Lord Jesus, I thank you for answered prayer, in Jesus name.

Leviathan Must Die

Bible Reading and Confession: Job 41:1–34

I Let them curse it that curse the day, who are ready to raise up their mourning. (Job 3:8)

In that day the Lord with his sore and great and strong sword shall punish leviathan the piercing serpent, even leviathan that crooked serpent; and he shall slay the dragon that is in the sea. (Isaiah 27:1)

There go the ships: there is that leviathan, whom thou hast made to play therein. (Psalm 104:26)

Thou brakest the heads of leviathan in pieces, and gavest him to be meat to the people inhabiting the wilderness. (Psalm 74:14)

Praise and Worship

Prayer Points

1. O Lord, arise and defend your interest in me, in the name of Jesus.
2. You the serpent in my foundation attacking my life, die, in the name of Jesus.
3. I destroy any power of leviathan working against my marriage, in the name of Jesus.
4. Serpent of destruction let the serpent of the Lord swallow you, in the name of Jesus.
5. O Lord, let the protection of leviathan be destroyed, in the name of Jesus.

6. Leviathan you have no place in my home, die, in the name of Jesus.

7. Serpent of destruction swallowing my blessings, vomit them and die, in the name of Jesus.

8. Any power using the spirit of leviathan to attack me, die, in the name of Jesus.

9. Let the power house of leviathan catch fire and burn to ashes, in the name of Jesus.

10. Leviathan, loose your boldness before me, in the name of Jesus.

11. I capture back my territory in the custody of leviathan, in the name of Jesus.

12. O Lord, deliver me and my household from any power that is too strong for us, in the name of Jesus.

13. Any power that is boasting against the power of God in my life, die, in the name of Jesus.

14. I destroy every plot of leviathan spirit against me and my family, in the name of Jesus.

15. Leviathan on assignment against my destiny, die, in the name of Jesus.

16. Leviathan on assignment against my calling and ministry, die, in the name of Jesus.

17. Leviathan on assignment against my Children, die, in the name of Jesus.

18. Leviathan on assignment against my health, die, in the name of Jesus.

19. Leviathan on assignment against my career, die, in the name of Jesus

20. I move out of the trap of leviathan by the fire of the Holy Ghost, in the name of Jesus.

21. I command the sword of the Lord, to locate the head of the evil leviathan on assignment against me, in the name of Jesus.

22. Lord Jesus, thank you for answered prayers, in the name of Jesus.

Deliverance from Satanic Oppression

Bible Reading and Confession

But upon mount Zion shall be deliverance, and there shall be holiness; and the house of Jacob shall possess their possessions. (Obadiah 1:17)

But thus saith the Lord, Even the captives of the mighty shall be taken away, and the prey of the terrible shall be delivered: for I will contend with him that contendeth with thee, and I will save thy children. (Isaiah 49:25)

In thee, O Lord, do I put my trust; let me never be ashamed: deliver me in thy righteousness. (Psalm 31:1)

Praise and Worship

Prayer Points

1. Father Lord, I thank you for your deliverance power, in the name of Jesus.
2. Lord Jesus, I thank you for your power that heals, in the name of Jesus.
3. Lord Jesus, I thank you for what you are going to do in my life today, in the name of Jesus
4. I drink the blood of Jesus and I eat the fire of the Holy Ghost, in the name of Jesus.
5. I break any demonic covenant existing in my foundation, in the name of Jesus.
6. I separate myself from occultic agreement in my family line, in the name of Jesus.

7. Serpentine power in my lineage, release me and die, in the name of Jesus.

8. I divorce any marriage to any spirit husband/wife both physically and spiritually, in the name of Jesus.

9. I vomit any evil deposit and plantation in my stomach, womb and blood stream, in the name of Jesus.

10. I renounce any evil association membership by fire, in the name of Jesus.

11. I destroy every power of evil dedication upon my life, in the name of Jesus.

12. I renounce any membership with any water spirit, in the name of Jesus.:

13. You power claiming right over my life, because of my parent involvement with you, release me now and die, in the name of Jesus.

14. Any man/women claiming right over my marriage, because of my parent agreement with you, today, I destroy your right and break your hold over my life, in the name of Jesus.

15. Every foundational power afflicting me because of my refusal to serve it, die, in the name of Jesus.

16. Powers of my father's house working against my progress, die, in the name of Jesus.

17. Any evil thing that entered my body because of the evil powers and covenants of my mother's house, die, in the name of Jesus.

18. I refuse to be a member of any demonic association existing in my lineage, in the name of Jesus.

19. I break loose from every collective captivity, in the name of Jesus.

20. Every evil thing I inherited from my parent unknowingly, die, in the name of Jesus.

21. Satan, hear it today, I am for Christ and not for you, in the name of Jesus.
22. Fire of God, incubate my life and make it untouchable for any evil powers, in the name of Jesus.
23. I renounce and revoke every unconscious covenant, I have entered with any power, I command them to break, in the name of Jesus.
24. Every witchcraft power in charge of my case, die, in the name of Jesus.
25. Strong man/woman of my family, die, in the name of Jesus.
26. Family idol and their custodians in my father's and mother's house, release me and die, in the name Jesus.
27. I refuse to operate under any known and unknown curses existing on my lineages, in the name of Jesus.
28. O Lord, possess me and use me for your glory in this world, in the name of Jesus.
29. Today, I declare the Lord Jesus Christ as the Lord over my life, in the name of Jesus.
30. I move out of captivity into glory, in the name of Jesus.
31. I receive power from the throne of grace to accomplish great things, in the name of Jesus.
32. Blood of Jesus, purge my system and make me whole, in the name of Jesus.
33. I repossess my virtues in satanic custody, in the name of Jesus.
34. I collect back my destiny from the hands of household wickedness, in the name of Jesus.
35. Judas in my family selling me out, commit suicide, in the name of Jesus.
36. Today, I receive my deliverance, in the name of Jesus.

37. I declare and decree no man/woman shall use my life to make wealth or obtain promotion, in the name of Jesus.

38. Covenant of poverty in my lineage, lose your potency over my life, in the name of Jesus.

39. Every arrow of untimely death fired at me, today go back to the sender, in the name of Jesus.

40. Father Lord, I thank you for my great deliverance, in the name of Jesus.

Let their Evil Counsellors Die

Bible Reading and Confession

And one told David, saying, Ahithophel is among the conspirators with Absalom. And David said, O Lord, I pray thee, turn the counsel of Ahithophel into foolishness. (2 Samuel 15:31)

And the counsel of Ahithophel, which he counselled in those days, was as if a man had enquired at the oracle of God: so was all the counsel of Ahithophel both with David and with Absalom. (2 Samuel 16:23)

Praise and Worship

Prayer Points

1. Let any evil counsel against me, fail woefully, in the name of Jesus.
2. Let the evil counsel against my home, fail woefully, in the name of Jesus.
3. Let the evil counsel of the powers of my father's house, against my career, fail woefully, in the name of Jesus.
4. Every evil counsel given by the kingdom of darkness against my life, back fire, in the name of Jesus.
5. O Lord, turn the witchcraft counsel against my Children into foolishness, in the name of Jesus.
6. Any mouth giving evil counsel against my life, be silence, forever, in the name of Jesus.
7. I command any Ahithophel of my calling to receive the stones of fire and die, in the name of Jesus.

8. I command the Ahithophel of my calling and ministry, to die, in the name of Jesus.

9. O Lord, disgrace every Ahithophel of my breakthrough, in the name of Jesus.

10. Lord Jesus, disgrace the Ahithophel at my place of work, in the name of Jesus.

11. Counsel of Ahithophel will no longer prosper in my family, in the name of Jesus.

12. O Lord, turn the wisdom of my Ahithophel into foolishness, in the name of Jesus.

13. Ahithophel of my father's house giving evil counsel against my life, die, in the name of Jesus.

14. O Lord, ridicule the Ahithophel in the camp of my enemy, in the name of Jesus.

15. Ahithophel that has refused my easy passage, commit suicide, in the name of Jesus.

16. Any power cooperating with the Ahithophel of my destiny, enough is enough, die, in the name of Jesus.

17. Evil reporters giving evil information about my household to the enemy, die, in the name of Jesus.

18. I command the fire of God on the gathering of Ahithophel, in the name of Jesus.

19. Every evil monitoring spirit of my father's house, your time is up, die, in the name of Jesus.

20. Lord God of Elijah, make me overcome every evil counsel given to frustrate my life, in the name of Jesus.

21. I decree, that the camp of my Ahithophel, shall come to not, in the name of Jesus.

22. Lord Jesus, I thank you for answered prayers, in Jesus name.

I Shall See My Desire Upon My Enemies

Bible Reading and Confession

Mine eyes also shall see my desire on mine enemies, and mine ears shall hear my desire of the wicked that rise up against me. (Psalm 92:11)

The Lord taketh my part with them that help me: therefore shall I see my desire upon them that hate me. (Psalm 118:7)

Praise and Worship

Prayer Points

1. I decree the rod of the wicked shall not rest upon my lot, in the name of Jesus.
2. I command the evil trap set by the enemies to catch the enemies now, in the name of Jesus.
3. Blood of Jesus, begin to cry against my enemies, in the name of Jesus.
4. I command every evil arrow of the enemy fired at me, to go back to the sender, in the name of Jesus.
5. O Lord, open my mouth over my enemies today, in the name of Jesus.
6. Every enemy of my destiny, perish in your Red sea by fire, in the name of Jesus.
7. Every disaster planned for me and my family this year, backfire, in the name of Jesus.
8. I decree, I shall see my desire on the enemies of my glory, in the name of Jesus.

9. I shall flourish and rule over the enemies of my life, in the name of Jesus.

10. Every plan of the enemy to frustrate my efforts, be wasted by fire, in the name of Jesus.

11. My good labor in every department of life, shall not be wasted, in the name of Jesus.

12. Lord Jesus, let those that hate me and seek my hurt, fall by the sword of their own enemies, in the name of Jesus.

13. I decree, my trust in the Lord shall be greatly rewarded, in the name of Jesus.

14. Any power hired to curse me, be cursed, in the name of Jesus.

15. Any satanic animal on assignment against me at the hours of the night, receive the arrows of fire and die, in the name of Jesus.

16. Caterpillar of the Most High God, bull doze my way to breakthrough, in the name of Jesus.

17. Any satanic power standing at the door, preventing my glory from speaking, die, in the name of Jesus.

18. Every wicked projection for my life, by any satanic power, die, in the of Jesus.

19. Satan, hear the word of the Lord, from today, you have no place in my life anymore, loose me and let me go, in the name of Jesus.

20. I decree, I shall see the glory of the Lord in my life this year, in the name of Jesus.

21. Any power planning for my funeral, receive your obituary, in the name of Jesus.

22. Darkness hear the word of the Lord, you shall not rule my day, in the name of Jesus.

23. I command the custodian of the idol of my father's house performing evil sacrifice on my behalf, to receive angelic slap, in the name of Jesus.
24. Fire of God, barricade my life and family from any satanic attack, in the name of Jesus.
25. I shall not inherit any evil plan against my father's house, therefore, die, in the name of Jesus.
26. I shall not inherit any wicked desire from my mother's house, therefore, die, in the name of Jesus.
27. Whatever is in my foundation attracting evil to my life, die, in the name of Jesus.
28. Lord Jesus, I thank you for answered prayers, in Jesus name.

Rain of Power

Bible Reading and Confession

But ye shall receive power, after that the Holy Ghost is come upon you: and ye shall be witnesses unto me both in Jerusalem, and in all Judaea, and in Samaria, and unto the uttermost part of the earth. (Acts 1:8)

Praise and Worship

Prayer Points

1. I receive power from on high to do exploit for Christ, in the name of Jesus.
2. O Lord, baptize me with power like on the day of Pentecost, in the name of Jesus.
3. Lord Jesus, take hold of my entire being and use it for your glory, in the name of Jesus.
4. Anything in me that will not allow me to do the will of God, die, in the name of Jesus.
5. I receive the spirit of boldness just as in the days of the apostles, in the name of Jesus.
6. Whatever is making me to rise and fall in the things of God, your time is up, die, in the name of Jesus.
7. I refuse to be a disgrace to the name of the Lord, in the name of Jesus.
8. O Lord, break me down and remold me to suit your purpose, in the name of Jesus.
9. I receive the anointing to be able to tarry, in the name of Jesus.

10. I decree from today, my life shall have positive impact on others, in the name of Jesus.
11. Holy Ghost make my body your place of abode, in the name of Jesus.
12. O Lord, release upon me today the power that made the apostles terrors to the kingdom of darkness, in the name of Jesus.
13. Spirit of Luke warmness in my life, come out and die, in the name of Jesus.
14. Holy Ghost, come upon me today and energize my spirit man, in the name of Jesus.
15. Holy Ghost, release into my life today signs and wonders, in the name of Jesus.
16. Any satanic power contending with the power of God in my life, die, in the name of Jesus.
17. The power to live a holy life, possess me, in the name of Jesus.
18. I destroy the throne of sin in my life, in the name of Jesus.
19. Anointing for great service onto the Lord, fall upon me, in the name of Jesus.
20. O Lord, separate me and let me stand out as one of your generals in this dispensation, in the name of Jesus.
21. Thank you father for answered prayers, in Jesus name.

Power to Get Wealth

Bible Reading and Confession

But thou shalt remember the Lord thy God: for it is he that giveth thee power to get wealth, that he may establish his covenant which he sware unto thy fathers, as it is this day. (Deuteronomy 8:18)

Praise and Worship

Prayer Points

1. I receive power from the throne of Grace to get wealth, in the name of Jesus.
2. God that works miracles, turn my financial life into a miracle, in the name of Jesus.
3. I reject the spirit of poverty, in the name of Jesus.
4. You the spirit that makes one to see good things and not obtain them, you have no place in my life, die, in the name of Jesus.
5. In the name of Jesus, from today, I shall be a giver and not a begger.
6. You rag of poverty in my lineage, you have no place in my life, be burnt to ashes, in the name of Jesus.
7. O Lord, reposition me to my rightful place, physically, spiritually and financially, in the name of Jesus.
8. I receive power from the throne of Grace to move into my promise land this year, in the name of Jesus.
9. I claim back my lost fertile ground, occupied by any fake lion, in the name of Jesus.

10. O Lord, from today, I refuse to remain the same, in the name of Jesus.

11. O Lord, use this prayer program to transform me and make me seat among the princes of nations, in the name of Jesus.

12. By the power in the name of Jesus, I receive my portion of the wealth of this state.

13. I claim and receive the anointing for good success, in the name of Jesus.

14. Every dry bone in my finances come alive, in the name of Jesus.

15. You the prince of Persia, wrestling with my angel of blessing, give up now and die, in the name of Jesus.

16. O God of promotion, promote me in every area of my life, in the name of Jesus.

17. O God of new beginning, let me experience your raw power in every department of my life, in the name of Jesus.

18. I receive the anointing for prosperity, in the name of Jesus.

19. My angel of blessing, locate me today, in the name of Jesus.

20. Every deeply rooted problem in my life, be uprooted by fire, in the name of Jesus.

21. I speak disgrace onto the spirit of failure in my life, in the name of Jesus.

22. I release my life from the control of desert spirit, in the name of Jesus.

23. I refuse to swim in the ocean of problems, in the name of Jesus.

24. Any power behind the problems of my life, die, in the name of Jesus.

25. Angels of blessings, begin to locate me for my own blessings now in this prayer program, in the name of Jesus.

26. Lord Jesus, I refuse to be kept busy by the devil, in the name of Jesus.

27. I receive power to close down any satanic factory, manufacturing problems for my life, in the name of Jesus.

28. Father Lord, I thank you for answered prayers, in the name of Jesus

My Home shall be a Testimony

Bible Reading and Confession

No evil shall befall you, nor shall any plague come near your dwelling.
(Psalm 91:10)

My people will dwell in a peaceful habitation, in secure dwellings, and in quiet resting places. (Isaiah 32:18)

Praise and Worship

Prayer Points

1. I declare and decree, there shall be no mourning in my home, in the name of Jesus.
2. I declare and decree, there shall be no sickness in my home, in the name of Jesus.
3. I declare and decree, there shall be no weeping in my home, in the name of Jesus.
4. I declare and decree, we shall not experience loss in my home, in the name of Jesus.
5. I declare and decree, no stranger shall invade my home, in the name of Jesus.
6. I command the blessings of God, that maketh rich and add no sorrow, to fall upon my home, in Jesus name.
7. My home shall be called blessed on earth, in the name of Jesus.
8. My home shall be on fire for God, in the name of Jesus.

9. My Children shall be like olive trees in my home, in the name of Jesus.

10. O Lord, lay your hands of power on my Children, in the name of Jesus.

11. My children's destiny shall not be perverted, in the name of Jesus.

12. My Children shall excel in their academic work and their lives, in the name of Jesus.

13. The spirit that destroy the lives of children in this country, shall not locate my children, in the name of Jesus.

14. From today, my home shall be known as the home of peace and joy, in the name of Jesus.

15. O Lord, I reject evil pattern in my home, in the name of Jesus.

16. O Lord, make my home a vehicle of salvation in this dispensation, in the name of Jesus.

17. Darkness shall not rule over my home, in the name of Jesus.

18. I declare and decree, there shall be no barrenness in my home, in the name of Jesus.

19. My Children shall be a source of joy to me and the kingdom of God, in the name of Jesus.

20. The devil will not harvest any soul in my home, in the name of Jesus.

21. Satan shall not have a hold over anyone in my home, in the name of Jesus.

22. Father Lord, I thank you for answered prayers, in the name of Jesus.

Prayer for Resurrection of Dry Bones

Bible Reading and Confession: Ezekiel 37

Praise and Worship

Prayer Points

1. Every dry bone in my life, come alive, in the name of Jesus.
2. Any power responsible for dryness in any area of my life, die, in the name of Jesus.
3. Every covenant of buried virtues in my life, break, in the name of Jesus.
4. Lord Jesus, bring me out of the valley to the mountain top, in the name of Jesus.
5. Every divine prophecy that is not active now, come alive now, in the name of Jesus.
6. Spirit of Pisgah in my life, die, in the name of Jesus.
7. Every financial embarrassement, die, in the name of Jesus.
8. I break every evil authority over my life, in the name of Jesus.
9. Evil altar, your day of judgement has come, die, in the name of Jesus.
10. I silence every satanic cry of evil prophets over my life, in the name of Jesus.
11. Fire of God, consume them that plan my downfall, in the name of Jesus.
12. I declare judgement against evil monitors, monitoring my life, in the name of Jesus.

13. Blood of Jesus, speak for me where I can not speak, in the name of Jesus.
14. I command this month and this year, to cooperate with my success, in the name of Jesus.
15. Father Lord, I thank you for answered prayers, in the name of Jesus.

Power to Un-Seat the Saul on the Throne of Your Destiny

Bible Reading and Confession: 1 Samuel 16:1–16,

And Saul cast the javelin ; for he said, I will smite David even to the wall with it. And David avoided out of his presence twice. And Saul was afraid of David, because the Lord was with him, and was departed from Saul.
(1Samuel 18:11–12)

And Saul sought to smite David even to the wall with the javelin: but he slipped away out of Saul's presence, and he smote the javelin into the wall: and David fled, and escaped that night. (1Samuel 19:10)

Praise and Worship

Prayer Points

1. Any King Saul, occupying the throne of my destiny, be unseated, in the name of Jesus.
2. Any power that wants to cut me off, die, in the name of Jesus.
3. Any power that is preventing me from being blessed in life, die, in the name of Jesus.
4. Powers following me around hindering my blessing, die, in the name of Jesus.
5. Powers following me around that wants to reduce me to nothing, die, in the name of Jesus.

6. Every adversaries of my father's house, ministering against me, be silenced, in the name of Jesus.

7. Spirit of error behind my problems, die, in the name of Jesus.

8. I refuse to cooperate with the enemies against myself, in the name of Jesus.

9. You, destructive spirit of my mother's house, that destroy the destiny of children born in to their family, die, in the name of Jesus.

10. Every activities of household wickedness against my life, fail woefully, in the name of Jesus.

11. I will not die as my parent died, in the name of Jesus.

12. I shall not eat from the dustbin of life, in name of Jesus.

13. Every curse of non achievement on my life, break now, in the name of Jesus.

14. Covenants of stagnation operating in my life, break, in the name of Jesus.

15. Herod of my destiny, die, in the name of Jesus.

16. Pharaoh of my divine promises, die, in the name of Jesus.

17. I shall occupy the throne of my destiny, in the name of Jesus.

18. Any power promoting shame and disgarce for me, fall by the sword of the Holy Spirit, in the name of Jesus.

19. Broom of destruction of the Lord, sweep away all my failures, rejection and problems, in the name of Jesus.

20. Every enemy of my divine reign, fall by your own sword, in the name of Jesus.

21. Every evil river flowing in my lineage, I cut you off from my life, in the name of Jesus.

22. Powers calling my name into disaster, you are a liar, die, in the name of Jesus.

23. I move from the valley of expectation to the mountain of testimony, in the name of Jesus.

24. Lord Jesus, call forth my glory from the grave of death, in the name of Jesus.

25. My glory hear the word of the Lord, arise and begin to speak, in the name of Jesus.

26. O Lord, awaken every sleeping anointing of greatness in me, in the name of Jesus.

27. I move from disappointment to divine appointment, in the name of Jesus.

28. I move from failure to success, in the name of Jesus.

29. I move from rejection to acceptance, in the name of Jesus.

30. Satanic stopper, you can not stop me, I will rise above my peers in and around me, in the name of Jesus.

31. Any power that dims glory in my father's and mother's house, stand still now, my glory and that of my children are not your lot, therefore, die, in the name of Jesus.

32. O Lord, I thank you for answered prayers, in the name of Jesus.

Loose Me and Let Me Go

Bible Reading and Confession: John 11

Praise and Worship

Prayer Points

1. Every power holding me down to failure, die, in the name of Jesus.
2. Powers of my father's house crying against my prosperity, die, in the name of Jesus.
3. Powers of my mother's house crying against my progress, die, in the name of Jesus.
4. O Lord, restore to me all my wasted years on this earth, in the name of Jesus.
5. Terminator assigned to terminate me, be terminated by fire, in the name of Jesus.
6. O Lord, move me forward by fire this year, in the name of Jesus.
7. Every power calling my name for evil at the hours of the night, die, in the name of Jesus.
8. I break myself loose from the hold of household idol, in the name of Jesus.
9. Spirit of almost there, working against my destiny, die, in the name of Jesus.
10. Thou wicked ancestral spirit, die, in the name of Jesus.
11. Let all diviners, divining evil against my life, be made powerless, in the name of Jesus.
12. I silence all negative words spoken and sealed in the heavenlies against me, in the name of Jesus.

13. I cancel every command binding me to the throne room of Satan, in the name of Jesus.

14. My enemies will acknowledge the finger of God in my life, in Jesus name.

15. Every satanic power fighting my testimonies, release me and die, in the name of Jesus.

16. Every Problems emenating from my mother's womb into my life, vanish, in Jesus name.

17. Every problems emanating from my father's lineage into my life, vanish, in the name of Jesus.

18. Every problems emanating from the usage of water into my life, vanish, in the name of Jesus.

19. Every problem emanating from the ground in to my life, vanish, in the name of Jesus.

20. Every problems emanating from the sun, moon and stars into my life, vanish, in the name of Jesus.

21. Any demon in charge of my case file in the spiritual realm, die, in the name of Jesus.

22. Any satanic power in my foundation magnetizing evil to me, die, in the name of Jesus.

23. I refuse for another to take my place in the journey of life, in the name of Jesus.

24. I refuse to operate at the tail region in my life, in the name of Jesus.

25. Any power programming rejection, disappointment and frustration into the sun, moon and star against me, die, in the name of Jesus.

26. Any satanic power pressing the sand for my sake, die, in Jesus name

27. Every witchcraft battle at the edge of my breakthrough, die, in the name of Jesus.

28. I refuse to obey satanic dictate for my life, in the name of Jesus.

29. Demons of poverty, release me and die, in the name of Jesus.

30. Demons of failures, release me and die, in the name of Jesus.

31. Demons of rejection, release me and die, in the name of Jesus.

32. Demons of disappointment in all areas of life, release me and die, in the name of Jesus.

33. Demons of profitless hardwork, release me and die, in the name of Jesus.

34. Demons of sicknesses, release me and die, in the name of Jesus.

35. Demons in charge of all kinds of problems, release me and die, in Jesus name.

36. Thank you Jesus for answered prayers, in Jesus name.

Prayer for Divine Intervention

Bible Reading / Confession:

And it came to pass, when men began to multiply on the face of the earth, and daughters were born unto them, That the sons of God saw the daughters of men that they were fair; and they took them wives of all which they chose. And the Lord said, My spirit shall not always strive with man, for that he also is flesh: yet his days shall be an hundred and twenty years. There were giants in the earth in those days ; and also after that, when the sons of God came in unto the daughters of men, and they bare children to them, the same became mighty men which were of old, men of renown. And God saw that the wickedness of man was great in the earth, and that every imagination of the thoughts of his heart was only evil continually. And it repented the Lord that he had made man on the earth, and it grieved him at his heart. And the Lord said, I will destroy man whom I have created from the face of the earth ; both man, and beast, and the creeping thing, and the fowls of the air; for it repenteth me that I have made them. But Noah found grace in the eyes of the Lord. (Genesis 6:1–8)

But God came to Abimelech in a dream by night, and said to him, Behold, thou art but a dead man, for the woman which thou hast taken ; for she is a man's wife. But Abimelech had not come near her: and he said, Lord, wilt thou slay also a righteous nation? (Genesis 20:3–4)

Praise and Worship

Prayer Points

1. O God of Abraham, where and whenever I need a voice to speak for me, Lord, Speak for me, in the name of Jesus.

2. I reject nightmare and sudden destruction, in the name of Jesus.

3. Every night and dream attack, scatter by fire, in the name of Jesus.

4. Every terror of the night, die, in the name of Jesus.

5. Encircle me, O Lord, with your wall of fire, in the name of Jesus.

6. Every Judas of my salvation, fall into your own trap, in the name of Jesus.

7. Christ of Gethsemane, intercede for me, in the name of Jesus.

8. O Lord, make me like the tree planted by the river side, in Jesus name.

9. I rise above every evil family root, in the name of Jesus.

10. O God of Elijah, deliver me from whatever is holding me down to this --------------- (Mention any unfavorable situation in your life) in Jesus name.

11. Holy Spirit, walk back to every second, minutes and hours of my life, claim for me, every good things I have lost due to ignorance, in the name of Jesus.

12. I reject the spirit of the tail and I claim the spirit of the Head, in the name of Jesus.

13. My life receive the fire of the Holy Ghost, in the name of Jesus.

14. Every foundational problem in my life, be destroyed by the fire of the Holy Ghost, in the name of Jesus.

15. I break every evil covenant, I have entered into consciously and unconsciously as a result of my past relationship, in the name of Jesus.

16. Every demonic curse placed upon me as a child, break, in the name of Jesus.

17. Any power of my mother's and father's house troubling my life, health, marriage and children, die, in the name of Jesus.

18. My life and that of any member of my household, shall not be used to obtain satanic promotion, in the name of Jesus.

19. O Lord, make me and every member of my family an untouchable coals of fire for the devil and his agents, in the name of Jesus.

20. Any satanic poison introduced into my body in the dream, I flush you out with the blood of the Jesus.

21. Any sickness that entered into my body as a result of sin, Lord Jesus, forgive me and remove it now, in the name of Jesus.

22. Every demonic covenant of untimely death in my life, as a result of my foundation, break, in the name of Jesus.

23. Any covenant that was entered into by my parent on my behalf, affecting my life and marriage, I renounce and reject you, break, in the name of Jesus.

24. Blood of Jesus, begin to speak healing, deliverance, salvation and prosperity into my life, in the name of Jesus.

25. Father Lord, I thank you for answered prayers, in the name of Jesus.

Prayer for Healing

Bible Reading and Confession:

Heal me, O LORD, and I will be healed; Save me and I will be saved, For You are my praise. (Jeremiah 17:14)

Surely our griefs He Himself bore, And our sorrows He carried ; Yet we ourselves esteemed Him stricken, Smitten of God, and afflicted. 5But He was pierced through for our transgressions, He was crushed for our iniquities ; The chastening for our well-being fell upon Him, And by His scourging we are healed.... (Isaiah 53:4–5)

But Jesus replied, "Every plant that My Heavenly Father has not planted will be pulled up by its roots. (Matthew 15:13)

Praise and Worship

Prayer Points

1. I command any dead organ in my body to come alive now, by the power of resurrection of the Lord Jesus Christ.
2. O Lord, lay your hand of healing upon my body, in the name of Jesus.
3. Christ of Calvary, let your healing stripes make me whole, in Jesus name.
4. Every fountain of sicknesses in my body, dry up, in the name of Jesus.

5. Let the divine fire of healing of the almighty God, begin to burn from the top of my head to the sole of my feet, in the name of Jesus.

6. I reject every unfavorable clinical prophecy made over me, by any doctor, in the name of Jesus.

7. You the root and habitation of cancer in my body, die, in the name of Jesus.

8. My body, hear the words of the Lord, receive strength, in the name of Jesus.

9. I command every root of diabetes in my life, die, in the name of Jesus.

10. I command every root of hypertension and any blood diseases in my body, to dry up, in the name of Jesus.

11. My body, hear the words of the living God, you shall not inhabit any form of sicknesses, in Jesus name.

12. Every inherited terminal dieases in my body, wither by fire, in the name of Jesus.

13. Balm of Gilead, make me whole, in the name of Jesus.

14. I drink the Blood of Jesus, for healing and deliverance in body, soul and spirit, in the name of Jesus.

15. God of Elijah, heal me and I shall be healed, in Jesus name.

16. I refuse whatever God has not created with me, that is manifesting in my life, in the name of Jesus.

17. The bible says, "everything created in the beginning by God was good" therefore, I command every organ in my body, return to the original state of creation, in the name of Jesus.

18. I shall not die before my time, in the name of Jesus.

19. Any power that wants to eat my flesh and drink my blood, be roasted, in the name of Jesus.

20. I shall not be used for satanic sacrifice, in the name of Jesus.

21. Every evil deposit in my body through food or water, be flushed out, by the blood of Jesus.

22. Father Lord, I thanks you for answered prayer, in the name of Jesus.

Prayer for Restoration

Bible Reading and Confession

And My people who are called by My name humble themselves and pray and seek My face and turn from their wicked ways, then I will hear from heaven, will forgive their sin and will heal their land. (2 Chronicles 7:14)

Then I will make up to you for the years That the swarming locust has eaten, the creeping locust, the stripping locust and the gnawing locust, My great army which I sent among you. (Joel 2:25)

Praise and Worship

Prayer Points

1. O Lord, forgive the sins of this nation and heal our Land, in the name of Jesus.
2. O Lord, restore this nation and all the people back to yourself, in the name of Jesus.
3. I break the stronghold of satan upon this nation and the people, in the name of Jesus.
4. O Lord, put men and women after your heart in the aim of affairs in this nation, in the name of Jesus.
5. Lord Jesus, by your mercy restore the economy of this nation, in the name of Jesus.
6. Every spirit of immorality in this nation, we bind you and cast you out from the lives of people of this nation, in the name of Jesus.

7. O Lord, put your spirit in our leaders in this nation, in the name of Jesus.

8. O Lord, remember your covenants with the forefathers of this nation, and restore your glory now, in the name of Jesus.

9. Every gathering against this nation in the kingdom of darkness, scatter, in the name of Jesus.

10. Every spirit of Sodom and Gomorrah in this nation, receive destruction, in the name of Jesus.

11. Any power seating on the promises of God in this nation and my life, die, in the name of Jesus.

12. My life, show forth the glory of God, in the name of Jesus.

13. Lord Jesus, mend the framented part of my life, in the name of Jesus.

14. With the Power of God, I disgrace every satanic battle in this nation, in the name of Jesus.

15. I move from where I am now to where Gad wants me to be, in the name of Jesus.

16. I shall not be counted among the failures in life, in the name of Jesus.

17. All those expecting my fall and disgrace, shall testify of God's goodness in my life, in the name of Jesus.

18. In the remaining years of my life, I shall be celebrated, in the name of Jesus.

19. Every yoke and affliction of our ancestral family, I am not your candidate, die, in the name of Jesus.

20. In this Year, as I look up to God, I shall not be ashamed, in the name of Jesus.

21. Christ the hope of Glory, shall make this year glorious for me and my household, in the name of Jesus.

22. Every good thing the enemy has declared impossible in my life, become possible by fire, in the name of Jesus.

23. I move forward by fire, in the name of Jesus.

24. Lord God of Elijah, give me dumbfounding breakthrough in this month, in the name of Jesus.

25. O Lord, as you made Sarah a laughter, make me a laughter, in the name of Jesus.

26. O Lord, as you open the mouth of Hannah over her enemies, all through this year open my mouth over all my enemies, in the name of Jesus.

27. In this year, I decree, I shall not see evil, in the name of Jesus.

28. Hear me, O yea land of ------------ (mention the state where you are), you must cooperate with my breakthrough, in the name of Jesus.

29. You the ground of this country, you shall not eat my flesh violently, in the name of Jesus.

30. You the ground of this country, hear the word of the living God, vomit my blessings you swallowed, in the name of Jesus.

31. Lord Jesus, I thank you for the answered prayers, in the Jesus name.

Bible Reading and Confession: Luke 1

Praise and Worship

Prayer Points

1.   Evil river flowing in my lineage causing diversion of my miracles, dry up now, in the name of Jesus.
2.   O Lord that answereth by fire, answer me by fire, in the name of Jesus.
3.   O God of comfort and joy, answer me by fire, in the name of Jesus.
4.   O God that changed the lot of Jabez, answer me by fire, in the name of Jesus.
5.   Lord Jesus, catapult me to greatness as you did for Daniel in a strange land, in the name of Jesus.
6.   I receive victory over the forces of wickedness, in the name of Jesus.
7.   I bind the strongman delegated to hinder the manifestation of my miracles, in the name of Jesus.
8.   I receive the mandate to put to flight every enemy of my breakthrough, in the name of Jesus.
9.   O Lord, let my path be cleared to the top by your hand of fire, in the name of Jesus.
10. O Lord, convert all my struggles to prosperity, in the name of Jesus.
11. Every evil preparation against my life be frustrated, in the name of Jesus.

12. I reject every inherited poverty and problems, in the name of Jesus.
13. I refuse to reap evil harvest from any department of my life, in the name of Jesus.
14. Blood of Jesus, disconnect my life from failure at the edge of breakthrough, in the name of Jesus.
15. Father Lord, I thank you for answered prayers, in the name of Jesus.

I Shall Be A Glory

Bible Reading and Confession: Psalm 8

You will also be a crown of beauty in the hand of the LORD,
And a royal diadem in the hand of your God. (Isaiah 62:3)

Praise and Worship

Prayer Points

1. O Lord, let new wells of blessings spring up for me in desert places, in the name of Jesus.
2. O Lord, bear me up on eagle's wings before my enemies, in the name of Jesus.
3. O Lord, anoint my eyes to see my divine opportunities, in the name of Jesus.
4. I refuse to allow my past to affect my future negatively, in the name of Jesus.
5. My years shall not be in struggles but prosperity, in the name of Jesus.
6. The mockery of my enemies shall result in my advancement, in the name of Jesus.
7. O Lord, turn my mourning to dancing, in the name of Jesus.
8. Any evil power employed to hinder my advancement, die, in the name of Jesus.
9. I command any evil hand pointing at my star at the hours of the night, wither, in the name of Jesus.
10. O Lord, convert my opposition to promotion, in the name of Jesus.

11. Any evil mouth raining incantation against my life, be silenced, in the name of Jesus.
12. O Lord, make my miracle invisible to my enemies, in the name of Jesus.
13. O Lord, build new wells of prosperity for me, in the name of Jesus.
14. I receive power to reap where I did not sow, in the name of Jesus.
15. I shall be a crown of glory in the hand of my God, in the name of Jesus.
16. Father Lord, I thank you for answered prayers, in the name of Jesus.

Bible Reading and Confession: Genesis:37

A man's enemies will be the members of his own household. (Matthew 10:36)

Praise and Worship

Prayer Points

1. Spoilers of dreams, you shall not locate my dreams, in the name of Jesus.
2. Every power of glory dimmer in my father's house, die, in the name of Jesus.
3. Any strange power looking for me to pervert my destiny, fall down and die, in the name of Jesus.
4. Every power of household wickedness attacking my dreams, die, in the name of Jesus.
5. I will not go according to the handwriting of the enemies, in Jesus name.
6. Any satanic pastor that have seen my divine dream and working against it, receive the stones of fire, in the name of Jesus.
7. Blood of Jesus, speak resurrection to my dead dreams, in the name of Jesus.
8. Any evil power that have taken over my dream, release it now and die, in the name of Jesus.
9. I command every demonic activity of household wickedness against my life, to be wasted by fire, in the name of Jesus.

10. Every Judas within and around me commit suicide by fire, in the name of Jesus.

11. Every evil decree by household wickedness to destroy me, fall to the ground and die, in the name of Jesus.

12. O Lord, arise and arrest any power assigned to arrest my destiny, in the name of Jesus.

13. My future is not for sale, therefore, any power bargaining with my future in my father's house, die, in the name of Jesus.

14. Any household wickedness that wants to use my life to obtain promotion, you are a liar, die, in the name of Jesus.

15. I command the evil powers of household wickedness, to swallow themselves, in the name of Jesus.

16. Father Lord, I thank you for answered prayers, in the name of Jesus.

Bible Reading and Confession

If the foundations are destroyed, What can the righteous do?
(Psalm 11:3)

Praise and Worship

Prayer Points

1. Spirit of Dagon standing against me from my foundation, die, in the name of Jesus.
2. Every strongman of the idol of my father's house, die, in the name of Jesus.
3. Every wicked agenda of the idols of my father's house in my life, be wasted, in the name of Jesus.
4. I silence every evil cry of the idols of my father's house over my destiny, in the name of Jesus.
5. Every idol power speaking against my destiny, die, in the name of Jesus.
6. The idols of my father's house seating on my finances, marriage and testimonies, die, in the name of Jesus.
7. Every wicked pronouncement of my family idol against any area of my life, be nullified, in the name of Jesus.
8. I recover all my blessings in the custody of any family idol, in the name of Jesus.
9. O Lord, do not look away from me, visit my foundation, in the name of Jesus.
10. I refuse to be used for any satanic sacrifice, in the name of Jesus.

11. Any problem that manifested in the life of my mother, my life is not your candidate, die, in the name.

12. Any problem that manifested in the life of my father, my life is not your candidate, die, in the name of Jesus.

13. Any sickness I inherited from any of my parent, die, in the name of Jesus.

14. I break away from bondages ensuring any problem in my lineage, in the name of Jesus.

15. I break and loose myself from the consequences of foundational idolatry, in the name of Jesus.

16. O Lord, I refuse to bear the punishment for the sins of my ancestors, in the name of Jesus.

17. The spirit of untimely death operating in my lineage, my life and that of my Children are not your candidate, die, in the name of Jesus.

18. Today, I repair my foundation with the blood of Jesus, in Jesus name.

19. Father Lord, I thank you for answered prayers, in the name of Jesus.

Destroying Anti-Breakthrough Forces

Bible Reading and Confession

Behold, I am the LORD, the God of all flesh; is anything too difficult for Me? (Jeremiah 32:27)

Praise and Worship

Prayer Points

1. Every wicked power that is working against my advancement, fall down and die, in the name of Jesus.
2. Every good thing presently eluding my life, flow back into it now, in the name of Jesus.
3. Father Lord, block every access that the powers of darkness have into my life with the blood of Jesus, in Jesus name
4. I receive the spirit of favor, in the name of Jesus.
5. O Lord, let men and women bless me any where I go, in the name of Jesus.
6. I decree the lot of the wicked shall not fall upon my life, in the name of Jesus.
7. I claim all my blessings by fire, in the name of Jesus.
8. I break every circle of failure in life, in the name of Jesus.
9. Any demonic power standing at the door of my breakthrough, collapse and die, in the name of Jesus.
10. Any witchcraft attack at the edge of my breakthrough, die, in the name of Jesus.

11. I claim the wealth that the death of Jesus Christ made available for me, in the name of Jesus.

12. Any satanic mountain of hindrance standing between me and my breakthrough, be destroyed by the thunder fire of God, in the name of Jesus.

13. I declare and decree, another man will not take my possessions, in the name of Jesus.

14. Any evil power using my life to negotiate for wealth, you are a liar, die, in the name of Jesus.

15. Every evil mark on my body causing failure at the edge of breakthrough, be erased with the blood of Jesus, in Jesus name.

16. Covenants of poverty in my lineage messing up my dreams, break, in the name of Jesus.

17. Every curse of none achievement issued against me, break, in the name of Jesus.

18. Every evil river flowing from my lineage linking me to failure, dry up, in the name of Jesus.

19. Spirit of almost there, that did not allow my parent to fulfill their dreams, in my life you are a liar, die, in the name of Jesus.

20. Father Lord, I thank you for answered prayers, in the name of Jesus.

I Shall Be a Fruitful Vine

Bible Reading and Confession:

God blessed them; and God said to them, "Be fruitful and multiply, and fill the earth, and subdue it; and rule over the fish of the sea and over the birds of the sky and over every living thing that moves on the earth. (Genesis 1:28)

Your wife shall be like a fruitful vine Within your house, your children like olive plants Around your table. (Psalm 128:3)

Praise and Worship

Prayer Points

1. O LORD, I thank you for the power of conception you have put in me, in the name of Jesus.
2. Lord Jesus, I thank you for your command that says, I should go into the world and multiply, in the name of Jesus.
3. Father Lord, I command every anti-conception powers in and around me, die, in the name Jesus.
4. You spirit husband / wife hindering my conception in the physical, fall down and die, in the name of Jesus.
5. O Lord, renew my youth and strength to be able to conceive and deliver like the Hebrew women, in the name of Jesus.
6. Every spiritual marriage existing between me and any spirit husband / wife, die, in the name of Jesus.

7. By the power in the name of Jesus, I receive the anointing to conceive and carry to full term without spotting, in Jesus name.

8. Any power that attack pregnancy in life at the hours of the night, die, in the name of Jesus.

9. Lord Jesus, put a smile on my face as you did for Hannah, in the name of Jesus.

10. You the spirit of barrenness, you have no place in my life, come out and die, in the name of Jesus.

11. In this year, I shall laugh over my enemies, in the name of Jesus.

12. Every covenant of barrenness or childlessness in my foundation working against the power of conception in my life, die, in the name of Jesus.

13. Any satanic blockage in my womb, be melted away by the fire of the Holy Ghost, in the name of Jesus.

14. Powers delaying my child bearing testimony, die, in the name of Jesus.

15. I receive the power of God to multiply in this year, in the name of Jesus.

16. O Lord, use my circle to confuse my enemies, in the name of Jesus.

17. O Lord, make me a laughter in this year, in the name of Jesus.

18. Father Lord, I thank you for answered prayers, in the name of Jesus.

Reversing the Evil Deeds of the Enemy

Bible Reading and Confession

He said to them, 'An enemy has done this.' The servants said to him, 'Do you want us then to go and gather them up?' (Matthew 13:28)

Praise and Worship

Prayer Points

1. I reverse any havoc done in my life by the powers of darkness, in the name of Jesus.
2. Any power that wants to bring my life to ridicule, die, in the name of Jesus.
3. Any power attacking me because of my father, die, in the name of Jesus.
4. I declare in the name of Jesus, my life is not for sale, in name of Jesus.
5. Any power attacking me becasue of my ancestral background of idolatry, die, in the of Jesus.
6. Any demonic power demanding for my worship, die, in the name of Jesus.
7. Covenants of lateness to the place of miracle in my life, die, in the name of Jesus.
8. I nullify every wicked agreement entered into by my forefathers, on behalf of all the children born into this family, in the name of Jesus.

9. Household wickedness from my father's house attacking me because of my father, die, in the name of Jesus.

10. Household wickedness, from my mother's house attacking me because of my mother, die, in the name of Jesus.

11. Satanic shrine abhorring my blessing, burn to ashes by the fire of God, in the name of Jesus.

12. Any evil power that allow one to see good things and not obtain them, die, in the name of Jesus.

13. I reject rejection in my life, in the name of Jesus.

14. I reject disappointment in my life, in the name of Jesus.

15. Any satanic power projecting frustration for me, die, in the name of Jesus.

16. Doors of my promotion and advancement, open by fire, in the name of Jesus.

17. O Lord, I thank you for answered prayers, in Jesus name.

The Sun Shall not Smite Me by Day and the Moon by Night

Bible Reading and Confession

The sun will not smite you by day, Nor the moon by night. The LORD will protect you from all evil; He will keep your soul.... (Psalm 121:6)

Praise and Worship

Prayer Points

1. Every wicked programming into the Sun against my life, die, in Jesus name.
2. Every wicked programming into the moon against me, die, in Jesus name.
3. Any satanic arrow stationed in the Sun against me, be melted by fire, in the name of Jesus.
4. Powers working in the stars to manipulate my destiny, die, in Jesus name.
5. Any satanic arrow station in the moon against me, be melted by fire, in the name of Jesus.
6. O Sun, hear the word of the Lord, from today you must not cooperate with my enemies against me, in the name of Jesus.
7. O moon, hear the word of the living God, you shall no longer obey any evil instruction against me, in the name of Jesus.
8. O Sun, vomit my blessings in you by fire, in the name of Jesus.

9. Every wicked astral projection into the Sun, moon and stars against my destiny, fail woefully, in the name of Jesus.

10. O Moon, vomit my blessings in you, in the name of Jesus.

11. Every affliction rising from the Sun, Moon and Stars into my life, be terminated, in the name of Jesus.

12. Any power in the second Heaven diverting my blessings, die, in Jesus name.

13. Any power programmed in the heavenlies to stop my Angels of blessings, die, in the name of Jesus.

14. Satanic tranquilizer of good things falling as dew upon my head from the heavenlies, dry up, in the name of Jesus.

15. Thank you Lord, for answered prayers, in Jesus name.

Bible Reading and Confession: Genesis 15

Praise and Worship

Prayer Points

1. Every problem emanating from the ground into my life, die, in the name of Jesus.
2. Every Problem introduced into my life by unfriendly friend, die, in the name of Jesus.
3. Every problem I used my mouth to call into my life, die, in the name of Jesus.
4. Every marital bliss assasinator assigned to kill the joy in my home, die, in the name of Jesus.
5. The health problem I inherited from my parent, die, in the name of Jesus.
6. Every financial problem I inherited from my lineage, die, in the name of Jesus.
7. Every problem I inherited from my mother's womb, die, in the name of Jesus.
8. I cancel and nullify every evil pronouncement from the mouth of satanic prophets against my life, in the name of Jesus.
9. I refuse to obey any satanic dictate for my life, in the name of Jesus.
10. My life, hear the word of the living God, you shall not obey any satanic command issued against you from any witchcraft coven, in the name of Jesus.

11. I withdraw every known and unknown cooperation, I have ever given to the devil and his agents over my life, in the name of Jesus.

12. I close every door of battle that I opened to the enemy with my hands, in the name of Jesus.

13. I break any evil covenant, I have entered into in the time of ignorance, in the name of Jesus.

14. Any power enforcing evil decree in my life, die, in the name of Jesus.

15. O Lord, make me your favorite, in Jesus name.

16. Satan, I command you to loose your grip over my life and family, in the name of Jesus.

17. I receive power to become that which the Lord, has declared for me to be, in the name of Jesus.

18. Jesus Christ of Nazareth, fight for me where they have gathered against me, in the name of Jesus.

19. Every problem emanating from the water and wind into my life, die in the name of Jesus.

20. Every root of problem in my life, wither, in the name of Jesus.

21. Every activities of demonic triangular powers over my life, be wasted by fire, in the nama of Jesus.

22. O Lord, take your position in my life and home, in the name of Jesus.

23. I command any problem that entered into my life through food, come out and die, in the name of Jesus.

24. Where men are failing, O Lord, give me the power to excel, in the name of Jesus.

25. Any gathering erecting satanic altar against me, scatter unto desolation, in the name of Jesus.

26. I reject and destroy every evil transfer through handshakes, in the name of Jesus.

27. I command any problem that came into my life through the exchange of clothings, die, in the name of Jesus.

28. Thank you, Lord Jesus for answered prayers, in Jesus name.

O Lord Thunder Over My Enemies

Bible Reading and Confession:

The LORD will go forth like a warrior, He will arouse His zeal like a man of war. He will utter a shout, yes, He will raise a war cry. He will prevail against His enemies. I have kept silent for a long time, I have kept still and restrained Myself. Now like a woman in labor I will groan, I will both gasp and pant.... (Isaiah 42:13–14)

An enemy did this,' he replied. So the servants asked him, '- Do you want us to go and pull them up? (Matthew 13:28)

Praise and Worship

Prayer Points

1. O Lord, arise in your anger and thunder over my enemies, in the name of Jesus.
2. O Lord, arise in your anger and disappoint the devices of the wicked fashioned against me, in the name of Jesus.
3. Lord Jesus, thunder over the enemies of my children, in the name of Jesus.
4. Thunder of God, arise in the greatness of your maker and scatter the camp of my adversaires unto desolation, in the name of Jesus.
5. Father Lord, let the cry of the wicked for mercy become an abomination before you, in the name of Jesus.
6. I command every wicked trap set for me by household wickedness, catch them, in the name of Jesus.

7. Every satanic attacker of my destiny from my father's house, receive the arrows of death, in the name of Jesus.

8. Every satanic attacker of my destiny form my mother's house, receive the arrows of death, in the name of Jesus.

9. Father Lord, in you anger prevail against any power limiting my potential, in the name of Jesus.

10. O Lord, arise and destroy all my enemies at once, in the name of Jesus

11. Any power, making life difficult for me, die, in the name of Jesus.

12. Lord Jesus, make my glory speak boldly and louder, in the name of Jesus.

13. Any power assigned to silence my glory, be silenced, in the name of Jesus.

14. From today, in the name of Jesus, I receive power to operate in my full potential, in Jesus name.

15. O Lord, let the cord of wickedness operating in my lineage, be broken by fire, in the name of Jesus.

16. I release the spirit of confusion into the camp of my enemies, in the name of Jesus.

17. Every satanic siege in any department of my life, expire by fire, in the name of Jesus.

18. Any power operating from any river making my ways slippery, drown now, in the name of Jesus.

19. Any mountain of problem in my life, be removed by fire, in the name of Jesus.

20. I receive divine mandate to move from this position to a higher ground, in the name of Jesus.

21. Every good thing the enemies have rendered useless in my life, come alive, in the name of Jesus.

22. I receive the power from on high to tread upon serpent and scorpions of my progress, in the name of Jesus.
23. Father Lord, I thank you for answered prayers, in the name of Jesus.

The Spear of the Wicked, shall go back to the Sender

Bible Reading and Confession:
1Samuel 17, 1Samuel 19:10–24

Saul hurled the spear for he thought, "I will pin David to the wall." But David escaped from his presence twice. Now Saul was afraid of David, for the Lord was with him but had departed from Saul.... (1Samuel 18:11–12)

Praise and Worship

Prayer Points

1. Father Lord, I thank you for your power of deliverance and protection, in the name of Jesus.
2. O Lord, I thank you for the power in the name of Jesus, that can set me free, in the name of Jesus.
3. Any power that have seen my star and wants to cage it, die, in the name of Jesus.
4. Any satanic altar erected against my advancement, you are a liar, be destroyed by fire, in the name of Jesus.
5. Every wicked spear of the enemy targeted against my life, backfire in the name Jesus.
6. Any satanic messenger on assignment against my home, be arrested by the Holy Ghost fire, in the name of Jesus.
7. O Lord, let every unrepentant adversaires of my life be naked permanently, after the order of king Saul, in Jesus name.

8. I decree the lot of the wicked shall not rest upon my life, in the name of Jesus.

9. Father Lord, let the evil plan of the enemy for my household become their lot, in the name of Jesus.

10. I command every wicked effort of satanic agent to pull me down, be wasted by fire, in the name of Jesus.

11. Any power that have decided to keep night vigil becasue of my household, die, in the name of Jesus.

12. Any power operating in the night to capture my destiny, die, in the name of Jesus.

13. Territorial agenda for my home because of God's hand upon me, die, in the name of Jesus.

14. Territorial forces fighting my rising, be silenced and die, in the name of Jesus.

15. Evil gathering summoned for my sake in order to silence me, be silenced and speak no more forever, in the name of Jesus.

16. Powers that follow me from my village to this place, I over turn your evil decision against my divine agenda, die, in the name of Jesus.

17. I shall not be wasted on my journey with destiny, in the name of Jesus.

18. I shall not be a wandering star in life, I shall occupy my position, in Jesus name.

19. O Lord, I receive by your power the anointing of excellence in every department of my life, in Jesus name.

20. Blood of Jesus, take my place in this battle; (mention any situation in your life) in the name of Jesus.

21. My life, whether you like it or not, you shall get the throne of your destiny, in the name of Jesus.

22. Thank you Lord Jesus, for answered prayers, in Jesus name.

Deliverance from the Hand of Strange Children and Deep Water

Bible Reading and Confession

Stretch forth Your hand from on high; Rescue me and deliver me out of great waters, Out of the hand of aliens. Whose mouths speak deceit, And whose right hand is a right hand of falsehood.… (Psalm 144:7–8)

Praise and Worship

Prayer Points

1. O Lord, deliver me from the hands of strange Children of darkness working against me, in the name of Jesus.
2. You strange Children in any body of water ministering against me, be silenced, in the name of Jesus.
3. Every enchantment of strange Children against my destiny, fall down to the ground and die, in the name of Jesus.
4. Any satanic command against my fruitfulness on earth from the mouth of strange Children, backfire by fire, in the name of Jesus.
5. Any strange mouth raining incantations against my name, be silenced forever, in the name of Jesus.
6. Lord Jesus, deliver me from the great waters of darkness used to monitor my life, in the name of Jesus.
7. Any power enchanting my name for evil in any deep waters, die, in the name of Jesus.

8. Every right hand of falsehood raised against me, wither by fire, in the name of Jesus.

9. You strange Children of darkness hindering the manifestation of my testimony, your time is over, die, in the name of Jesus.

10. I withdraw every conscious and unconscious cooperation with strange Children of darkness, in the name of Jesus.

11. Any strange child of darkness diverting my blessings, your time is up, die, in the name of Jesus.

12. I break every legal hold of strange Children in my life, in the name of Jesus.

13. O Lord, stretch forth thy hand from above and bring me out of deep waters, that have been holding me captive, in the name of Jesus.

14. I break myself loose from collective captivity of strange Children in my family, in the name of Jesus.

15. Satanic deep waters abhorring my blessings, dry up now and release my blessings, in the name of Jesus.

16. Every falsehood of strange Children in my life, expire by fire, in the name of Jesus.

17. Owners of evil load in my life, carry your load by fire, in the name of Jesus.

18. Let God arise and let all the strange Children involve in afflicting my life, be scattered, in the name of Jesus.

19. O Lord, make mockery of the gathering of strange Children over my life, in the name of Jesus.

20. I shall not be a prey to strange Children in my father's house and my mother's house, in the name of Jesus.

21. Every strange water flowing from my lineage into my life, dry up by fire, in the name of Jesus.

22. Any demonic deep waters assigned to carry away my blessings, your day of judgement is now, dry up by fire, in the name of Jesus.

23. I command every demonic deep water, loose your potency over my life, in the name of Jesus.

24. I recover all my blessings in any demonic deep waters, in the name of Jesus.

25. Any of my blessings confiscated by demonic strange Children, be released by the fire of the Holy Ghost, in the name of Jesus.

26. Any demonic deep waters that wants to swallow me, you are a liar, dry up by fire, in the name of Jesus.

27. O Lord, cause chaos in the camp of demonic strange Children working against me, in the name of Jesus.

28. Father Lord, I thank you for answered prayers, in the name of Jesus.

Bible Reading and Confession

and say, 'Thus says the Lord GOD, "Woe to the women who sew magic bands on all wrists and make veils for the heads of persons of every stature to hunt down lives! Will you hunt down the lives of My people, but preserve the lives of others for yourselves? For handfuls of barley and fragments of bread, you have profaned Me to My people to put to death some who should not die and to keep others alive who should not live, by your lying to My people who listen to lies.... Therefore, thus says the Lord GOD, Behold, I am against your magic bands by which you hunt lives there as birds and I will tear them from your arms; and I will let them go, even those lives whom you hunt as birds. I will also tear off your veils and deliver My people from your hands, and they will no longer be in your hands to be hunted; and you will know that I am the LORD.... (Ezekiel 13:18-21)

Our soul has escaped as a bird out of the snare of the trapper; The snare is broken and we have escaped. (Psalm 124:7)

Praise and Worship

Prayer Points

1. Any power hunting for my soul, fall down and die, in the name of Jesus.
2. Any power that seeks for the souls of my Children to kill them, die, in the name of Jesus.

3. I shall not be used for satanic sacrifice, in the name of Jesus.

4. Satanic powers that cages souls, my soul and that of my Children are not your lot, die, in the name of Jesus.

5. Satanic power in the area that I live seeking for the souls of men, you shall not locate my house, in the name of Jesus.

6. Any satanic trap set for my soul, you shall not catch me, trap your owner, in the name of Jesus.

7. Any part of my life in the cage of soul hunters, be released by fire, in the name of Jesus.

8. Lord Jesus, speak for me, where I cannot speak for myself, in the name of Jesus.

9. I render useless, the power of soul hunters assigned against me, in the name of Jesus.

10. Any soul hunters assigned against me, commit suicide, in the name of Jesus.

11. I command my soul and that of my Children, to become hot coals of fire, in the name of Jesus.

12. I reverse any evil covenant of wastage made over my life, in the name of Jesus.

13. Every soul hunters in my father's house, receive the stones of fire, in the name of Jesus.

14. Every soul hunters in my mother's house, receive the stones of fire, in the name of Jesus.

15. Any soul hunter pretending to be my friend, O Lord, expose and disgrace them, in the name of Jesus.

16. O Lord, empower me to win the battle against soul hunters in my family, in the name of Jesus.

17. I withdraw my life from the control of soul hunters, in the name of Jesus.

18. O Lord, cause a mighty confusion in the camp of soul hunters against my life, in the name of Jesus.
19. O Lord, Kill the soul hunters against the life of my Children, in the name of Jesus.
20. Father Lord, I thank you for answered prayers, in the name of Jesus.

Bible Reading and Confession

I have seen slaves riding on horses and princes walking like slaves on the land. (Ecclesiastes 10:7)

Praise and Worship

Prayer Points

1. Any power that wants to turn my prince into a slave, die, in the name of Jesus.
2. Any power on assignment to turn my glory into dust, die, in the name of Jesus.
3. I refuse satanic trade and barter with my glory, in the name of Jesus.
4. Every destiny perverting powers on assignment against my destiny, die, in the name of Jesus.
5. Satanic powers on assignment to waste my destiny, be wasted by fire, in the name of Jesus.
6. Spirit of disgrace in my foundation attacking my destiny, die, in the name of Jesus.
7. Spirit of non-achievement in my foundation attacking my destiny, die, in the name of Jesus.
8. Every power of glory dimmers in my lineage, my glory is not your candidate, die, in the name of Jesus.
9. Wasters of potentials, you shall not waste my potentials, die, in the name of Jesus.
10. Any power assigned to make my life a ridicule, you are a liar, die, in the name of Jesus.

11. I come out of obscurity into lime light, in the name of Jesus.

12. Any power that have vowed, that, they will not see me rise and shine, you are a liar, die, in the name of Jesus.

13. Any power pinning down my destiny, preventing it from speaking, be wasted, in the name of Jesus.

14. Any power raining demonic incantation against my destiny, die, in the name of Jesus.

15. O Lord, help me to seat on the throne of my destiny, in the name of Jesus.

16. I move out of every demonic cage of limitation, in the name of Jesus.

17. Any power using my destiny to obtain promotion, die, in the name of Jesus.

18. I command life in to any area of my destiny that the enemies have perverted, in the name of Jesus.

19. O Lord, fight the battle of destiny for my life, in the name of Jesus.

20. Every dark cloud surrounding my destiny, be dispersed by fire, in the name of Jesus.

21. I decree as a prince, I shall rule and not be ruled over, in the name of Jesus.

22. I decree as a prince, I shall not beg for bread, I shall be a blessing, in the name of Jesus.

23. Father Lord, I thank you for answered prayers, in the name of Jesus.

I Withdraw My Name from the Calendar of Tragedy

Bible Reading and Confession:

For they intended evil against thee: they imagined a mischievous device, which they are not able to perform. (Psalm 21:11)

Praise and Worship

Prayer Points

1. Any power behind frustration in my life, die, in the name of Jesus.
2. I destroy every satanic book of destruction opened against me, in the name of Jesus.
3. I destroy every satanic book of untimely death opened against me, in the name of Jesus.
4. I destroy every satanic book of failure opened against me, in the name of Jesus.
5. I destroy every satanic book of accident opened against me, in the name of Jesus.
6. I destroy every satanic book of terminal illness opened against me, in the name of Jesus.
7. Any power responsible for calamity in this season, you shall not locate my house, in the name of Jesus.
8. Every calendar of tragedy designed for me and my household, catch fire and burn to ashes, in the name of Jesus.

9. I command any satanic vehicle of destruction set in motion against me, to breakdown, in the name of Jesus.

10. Satan, hear the word of the living God, "for I and the children that the Lord have given to me are for signs and wonders," therefore, I command you to take your hands off the affairs of my family, in the name of Jesus.

11. Thank you Lord for answered prayers, in Jesus name.

O Lord, Open My Mouth Over My Enemy

Bible Reading and Confession

And Hannah prayed, and said, My heart rejoiceth in the LORD, mine horn is exalted in the LORD: my mouth is enlarged over mine enemies; because I rejoice in thy salvation. (1 Samuel 2:1)

When the LORD turned again the captivity of Zion, we were like them that dream. Then was our mouth filled with laughter, and our tongue with singing: then said they among the heathen, The LORD hath done great things for them. (Psalm 126:1–2)

Till he fill thy mouth with laughing, and thy lips with rejoicing. (Job 8:21)

Praise and Worship

Prayer Points

1. O Lord, command the season of my laughter to manifest now by fire, in Jesus name.
2. I command my season of abundance to come forth by fire, in the name of Jesus.
3. O God of Multitude, perform multiple miracles in my life in this month, in the name of Jesus.
4. Any power that is benefiting from my problems, die, in the name of Jesus.
5. Any power using my life to obatin any demonic promotion, be wasted by fire, in the name of Jesus.

6. In this season, O Lord, I receive power to laugh my enemies to scorn, in the name of Jesus.

7. I command, in the name of Jesus, everything that have been working against me to begin to work for me, in the name of Jesus.

8. Any problem expander in and around me your end has come, die, in the name of Jesus.

9. O Lord, I command the source of Joy of all my enemies to become their source of sorrow, in the name of Jesus.

10. Every demonic mountain surrounding my life, collapse after the order of Jericho, in the name of Jesus.

11. Every child of perdition around me making life difficult for me, be exposed and be disgraced, in the name of Jesus.

12. Powers causing failure at the edge of my breakthrough, die, in the name of Jesus.

13. I receive power from on high to be above always, in the name of Jesus.

14. Father Lord, open my mouth wide over my enemies this month, in the name of Jesus.

15. Father Lord, I thank you for answered prayers, in Jesus name.

O Lord, Put Me on the Mountain of Bashan (Fruitfulness)

Bible Reading and Confession: Numbers 21

The hill of God is as the hill of Bashan; an high hill as the hill of Bashan.
Why leap ye, ye high hills? this is the hill which God desireth to dwell in; yea, the LORD will dwell in it for ever. (Psalm 68:15–16)

Praise and Worship

Prayer Points

1. By the power in the name of Jesus, I come out of frustration, depression, disappointment, and rejection, in the name of Jesus.
2. Powers suspending my glory, release me and die, in the name of Jesus.
3. Powers responsible for delayed miracles in my life, die, in the name of Jesus.
4. Power responsible for marital failures in my life, die, in the name of Jesus.
5. Powers responsible for financial failure in my life, die, in the name of Jesus.
6. Powers resposible for career failure in my life, die, in the name of Jesus.
7. Powers responsible for business failure in my life, die, in the name of Jesus.

8. I receive power from on high, to occupy my mountain of fruitfulness (mountain of Bashan), in the name of Jesus.

9. Satanic Judas around me, selling me out to the enemies, die, in the name of Jesus.

10. Powers causing defeat in my life, receive the stones of fire, in the name of Jesus.

11. O Lord, let the vessel carrying my blessings dock in my house today, in the name of Jesus.

12. Any power that has vowed, that I will not sing my song and dance my dance in this year, expire before the end of today, in Jesus name.

13. Angels that deliver blessings, my life is ready, locate me by fire, in the name of Jesus.

14. Father Lord, I thank you for answered prayers, in the name of Jesus.

Breaking Satanic Curses of Hardship Placed on the Ground for my sake

Bible Reading and Confession:

And the Lord said unto Cain, Where is Abel thy brother? And he said, I know not: Am I my brother's keeper? And he said, What hast thou done? the voice of thy brother's blood crieth unto me from the ground. And now art thou cursed from the earth, which hath opened her mouth to receive thy brother's blood from thy hand; When thou tillest the ground, it shall not henceforth yield unto thee her strength; a fugitive and a vagabond shalt thou be in the earth. (Genesis 4:9–12)

And unto Adam he said, Because thou hast hearkened unto the voice of thy wife, and hast eaten of the tree, of which I commanded thee, saying, Thou shalt not eat of it: cursed is the ground for thy sake; in sorrow shalt thou eat of it all the days of thy life; Thorns also and thistles shall it bring forth to thee; and thou shalt eat the herb of the field; In the sweat of thy face shalt thou eat bread, till thou return unto the ground; for out of it wast thou taken: for dust thou art, and unto dust shalt thou return. (Genesis 3: 17–19)

Praise and Worship

Prayer Points

1. Father, I thank you for your word, which says; **As the bird go by wandering, as the swallow by flying, so the curse causeless shall not come. (Proverbs 26:2)**

2. Lord Jesus, I thank you for your power that can break every evil curse, in the name of Jesus.

3. Evil decree against me in this land, I cancel you with the blood of Jesus.

4. Powers issuing satanic curse on this land because of me, die, in the name of Jesus.

5. Curses sent ahead of me before my arrival in this land, break, in the name of Jesus.

6. Any power that arrived this country before my arrival with the mandate to enforce any satanic curse in my life, die, in the name of Jesus.

7. Curses making life hard for me in this land, break, in the name of Jesus.

8. Every evil decree against my life to return home as I came, die, in the name of Jesus.

9. I decree by the anointing of the man of Galilee, you this land, you shall yield your strength to me, in the name of Jesus.

10. Powers behind strange curses in my life, die, in the name of Jesus.

11. Any personality waiting for my return without any testimony, receive disgrace, in the name of Jesus.

12. Any satanic agent boasting for my downfall, receive the arrows of destruction, in the name of Jesus.

13. Powers in this land carrying out evil assignment against me, what are you waiting for? Die! in the name of Jesus.

14. O God of speedy recovery, recover my life from laboring under any satanic curses, in the name of Jesus.

15. My potential and virtues under satanic curse of hardship, arise and break lose, in the name of Jesus.

16. My life hear the word of the Lord, begin to experience milk and honey, in this land, in the name of Jesus.

17. You desert spirit attacking my career and business in this land, die, in the name of Jesus.

18. Blood of Jesus, break me free from any satanic curses afflicting my handy work in this land, in the name of Jesus.

19. I shall experience bountiful harvest in this land whether I like it or not, in the name of Jesus.

20. I thank you Jesus for answered prayers, in the name of Jesus.

Bible Reading and Confession:

And the Lord said unto him, Therefore whosoever slayeth Cain, vengeance shall be taken on him sevenfold. And the Lord set a mark upon Cain, lest any finding him should kill him. (Genesis 4:15)

They gather themselves together, they hide themselves, they mark my steps, when they wait for my soul. (Psalm 56:6)

Praise and worship

Prayer Points

1. Any satanic mark of failure placed upon my forehead, I erase it with the blood of Jesus.
2. Any satanic mark of almost there placed upon my body, I erase it with the blood of Jesus.
3. Any satanic mark of rejection upon my body, I erase it, with the blood of Jesus.
4. Any satanic mark of disappointment on my body, I erase it with the blood of Jesus.
5. I erase any mark of poverty place upon my body, with the blood of Jesus.
6. I erase any mark of disfavor place upon my body, with the blood of Jesus.
7. I erase any mark of stagnancy place upon my body, with the body of Jesus.
8. I erase any mark of untimely death place upon my body, with the blood of Jesus.

9. Marks of reproach lose your potency upon my life, in the name of Jesus.

10. Marks of hatred lose your potency upon my life, in the name of Jesus.

11. Marks of disgrace lose your potency upon of life, in the name of Jesus.

12. Powers responsible for evil marks in my life, die, in the name of Jesus.

13. I soak myself inside the blood of Jesus, in the name of Jesus.

14. I put upon my body the mark of the blood of Jesus, in the name of Jesus.

15. I decree the trap of the enemy will not capture me, in the name of Jesus.

16. O Lord, favor me in this prayer section, in the name of Jesus.

17. Powers pressing down my head, you are a liar, release me and die, in the name of Jesus.

18. Powers using satanic marks to control my life, die, in the name of Jesus.

19. Oil of favor baptize me throughout this year, in the name of Jesus.

20. Satanic marks assigned to stop me this year, lose your potency, in the name of Jesus.

21. Father Lord, I thank you for answered prayers, in the name Jesus.

Bible Reading and Confession: Daniel 6

Therefore, because the king's commandment was urgent, and the furnace exceeding hot, the flames of the fire slew those men that took up Shadrach, Meshach, and Abednego. And these three men, Shadrach, Meshach, and Abednego, fell down bound into the midst of the burning fiery furnace. Then Nebuchadnezzar the king was astonished, and rose up in haste, and spake, and said unto his counsellors, did not we cast three men bound into the midst of the fire? They answered and said unto the king, True, O king. (Daniel 3:22-24)

Praise and Worship

Prayer Points

1. Every satanic gathering planning evil against me, receive confusion, in the name of Jesus.
2. Any satanic group planning my death, die in my place, in the name of Jesus.
3. Satanic decision taking against me, back fire, in the name of Jesus.
4. Spirit of error, possess the camp of my enemies, in the name of Jesus.
5. By the power in the blood of Jesus, I escape the rod of the wicked, in the name of Jesus.
6. Demon of jealousy of my father's house, instigating people against me, die, in the name of Jesus.

7. I decree the fire of the enemy shall not burn me, in the name of Jesus.

8. I decree the lie of the enemy against me shall cause my elevation, in the name of Jesus.

9. All those that seek my destruction shall fall for my sake, in the name of Jesus.

10. O Lord, twist the tongue of the enemy to begin to speak in my favor, in the name of Jesus.

11. Evil covenants of non-achievement of my mother's house, causing the enemy to come against me at the verge of breakthrough, break, in the name of Jesus.

12. Every evil trap set for me by the enemy, fail to capture me, in the name of Jesus.

13. I will not die as planned by the enemy, I will live my life to the fullest in Christ Jesus, in the name of Jesus.

14. Household powers causing external battles for me always, die, in the name of Jesus.

15. Every executor of satanic plan in my life, you are a liar, die, in the name of Jesus.

16. Instrument of Satanic executor fashioned against me, back fire, in the name of Jesus.

17. Satanic executor assigned to kill me, turn around now in the name of Jesus, kill your sender, in the Jesus name.

18. Powers that want to kill me because of God's favor upon my life, die, in the name of Jesus.

19. Satanic Judge / king in-charge of my case, I command you to speak for me, in the name of Jesus.

20. O Lord, show the satanic Judge / king visions that will put terrifying fear in them, in the name of Jesus.

21. Father Lord, I thank you, for answered prayer, in the name of Jesus.

Power Against the Spirit of Pisgah (Almost There)

Bible Reading and Confession: Deuteronomy 34:1–12

Praise and Worship

Prayer Points:

1. Powers at the entrance of my promise land preventing me from entering, die, in the name of Jesus
2. Powers that make one to see good things and not possess it, die, in the name of Jesus.
3. I shall not die at the edge of my breakthrough, in the name of Jesus.
4. Spirit of Pisgah shall not be victorious over my life, in the name of Jesus.
5. I receive power to see and possess my possessions in the name of Jesus.
6. O Lord, do not give up on me help me to finish well, in the name of Jesus.
7. I shall not die while still struggling, in the name of Jesus.
8. I shall not start and not finish it, in the name of Jesus.
9. I shall not build for another to take over, in the name of Jesus.
10. Another man will not take my position in life, in the name of Jesus.
11. Power of almost there, I terminate your activities in my life, in Jesus name.

12. O Lord, help me to start well and finish well, in the name of Jesus.
13. Powers that cut one off before the day of glory, you shall not succeed in my life, die, in the name of Jesus.
14. Powers that make one to invest and not reap the reward, over my life, you are a liar, die, in the name of Jesus.
15. I decree that the good works which the Lord has begun in my life, the hand of the Lord shall finish it, in Jesus name.
16. I shall not be a hindrance to my promise land, in the name of Jesus.
17. Whatever will make God replace me with another, die, in Jesus name.
18. O Lord, do not forsake the work of thine hand, in the name of Jesus.
19. Another will not reap my harvest, in the name of Jesus.
20. I will not leave this world in a hurry, in the name of Jesus.
21. Father Lord, thank you for answered prayers, in the name of Jesus.

Deliverance from the Power of the Night

Bible Reading and Confession:

He who dwells in the secret place of the Most High Shall abide under the shadow of the Almighty. I will say of the Lord, "He is my refuge and my fortress; My God, in Him I will trust." Surely, He shall deliver you from the snare of the fowler[a] And from the perilous pestilence. He shall cover you with His feathers, And under His wings you shall take refuge; His truth shall be your shield and buckler. You shall not be afraid of the terror by night, Nor of the arrow that flies by day, Nor of the pestilence that walks in darkness, Nor of the destruction that lays waste at noonday. (Psalm 91:1-6)

Praise and Worship

Prayer Points

1. Powers that operate at night to attack me, die, in the name of Jesus.
2. Powers of darkness that feeds me with evil food at night, die, in the nameof Jesus.
3. I vomit every satanic poison in my system, introduce into my body at the hours of the night, in the name of Jesus.
4. Powers using the night to attack my destiny, die, in the name of Jesus.
5. Powers using the night to carry out evil assignment against me, die, in the name of Jesus.

6. I decree the night shall not be my caldron, in the name of Jesus.

7. Pot of darkness cooking my affairs at the hours of the night, break, in the name of Jesus.

8. Powers using the night to rob me of my joy, die, in the name of Jesus.

9. Night vomit everything you have stolen from me, in the name of Jesus.

10. Witchcraft meeting summoned for my sake at night, shall not hold, in the name of Jesus.

11. Witchcraft gathering against me at night, scatter, in the name of Jesus.

12. Anywhere my name is mentioned for evil in the night, thunder of God answer them, in the name of Jesus.

13. Powers calling my head for evil at the hours of the night, die, in the name of Jesus.

14. Powers passing evil judgement against me at the hours of the night, die, in the name of Jesus.

15. Any power sending evil command against my day at the hours of the night, die, in the name of Jesus.

16. Powers that uses the night to arrest my progress and success for the next day, die, in the name of Jesus.

17. Spirit of bad luck assigned to follow me around the next day at the hours of the night, die, in the name of Jesus.

18. I decree, I shall not answer any evil call at the hours of the night, in the name of Jesus.

19. I collect back by fire all my goods confiscated at the hours of the night, by the power in the blood of Jesus.

20. I cancel any demonic exchange that took place in my life at the hours of the night, in the name of Jesus.

21. Satanic cages of the night, release my destiny, in the name of Jesus.
22. Satanic cages of the night, release my star, in the name of Jesus.
23. Satanic cages of the night, release my potentials, in the name of Jesus.
24. Satanic cages of the night, release my health, in the name of Jesus.
25. Satanic cages of the night, release my wealth, in the name of Jesus.
26. Satanic cages of the night, release my children, in the name of Jesus.
27. Satanic cages of the night, release my womb, in the name of Jesus.
28. Satanic cages of the night, release my wife / husband, in the name of Jesus.
29. Satanic cages of the night, release my promotion, in the name of Jesus.
30. Altars of the night, abhorring anything that belong to me, release it now and catch fire, in the name of Jesus.
31. Thank you, Lord, for answer to my prayer.

Destroying the Sword and the Bow of the Wicked

Bible Reading and Confession:

The wicked have drawn out the sword, and have bent their bow, to cast down the poor and needy, and to slay such as be of upright conversation. (Psalm 37:14)

Praise and Worship

Prayer Points

1. O Lord, I thank you for the power of an overcomer, in the name of Jesus.
2. Father Lord, I thank you for you will give me victory over the sword and the bow of the wicked operating in my vicinity, in the name of Jesus.
3. I command the bow of destruction of the wicked set in motion against me, to catch fire and burn to ashes, in the name of Jesus.
4. Sword of impotency of the wicked fashioned against my husband, die, in the name of Jesus.
5. Bow of Miscarriage, the enemy is using to terminate pregnancy in my life, back fire, in the name of Jesus.
6. Sword and Bow of the wicked operating in my environment, you shall not locate my house, go back to your sender, in the name of Jesus.
7. Bow of bareness fashioned against my home, back fire, in the name of Jesus.

8. Sword of the wicked fashioned to destroy my household, die, in the name of Jesus.

9. Sword of untimely death lifted-up to the heavenlies against any member of my household, go back to your sender, in the name of Jesus.

10. Bows of Poverty released against my finances, die, in the name of Jesus.

11. Sword of Divorce of the wicked released against my marriage, die, in the name of Jesus.

12. Arrows of failure of the wicked fired against my children, go back to your sender, in the name of Jesus.

13. Sword of frustration of the wicked buried in the ground against my life, be exhumed by fire, in the name of Jesus.

14. Bow of sickness of the wicked fired into my body at the hours of the night, go back to your sender, in the name of Jesus.

15. Bow of rejection of the wicked fashioned against my life, die, in the name of Jesus.

16. Bow of disappointment of the wicked fashioned against my life, die, in the name of Jesus.

17. Anti-marriage sword of the wicked released against my marital life, die, in the name of Jesus.

18. O Lord, put songs of victory in my mouth this month, in the name of Jesus.

19. I decree no weapon of the wicked fashioned against me shall prosper, in the name of Jesus.

20. My body, soul and spirit, reject any weapon of the wicked fashioned against you, in the name of Jesus.

21. Bow of dream attack of the wicked fashioned against me, die, in the name of Jesus.

22. Father Lord, I thank you for answered prayer, in the name of Jesus.

Confessions:

But upon mount Zion there shall be deliverance, and there shall be holiness; and the house of Jacob shall possess their possessions. (Obadiah 1:17)

But thus says the Lord, Even the captives of the mighty shall be taken away, and the prey of the terrible be delivered; For I will contend with him who contends with you, And I will save thy children. I will feed those who oppress you with their own flesh, and they shall be drunk with their own blood as with sweet wine. All flesh shall know That I, the Lord, am your Savior, And your Redeemer, the Mighty One of Jacob. (Isaiah 49: 25–26)

But he answered and said, every plant, which my heavenly Father hath not planted, shall be rooted up. (Matthew 15:13)

If my people, which are called by my name, shall humble themselves, and pray, and seek my face, and turn from their wicked ways; then will I hear from heaven, and will forgive their sin, and will heal their land. (2Chronicles 7:14)

For the Lord God is a sun and shield: The Lord will give grace and glory: no good thing will he withhold from them that walk uprightly. (Psalm 84:11)

Lo, children are a heritage of the Lord: and the fruit of the womb is his reward. As arrows are in the hand of a mighty man; so are children of the youth. Happy is the man that hath his quiver full of them: they shall not be ashamed, but they shall speak with the enemies in the gate. (Psalm 127:3–5)

He maketh the barren woman to keep house, and to be a joyful mother of children. Praise ye the Lord. (Psalm 113:9)

But thou shalt remember the Lord thy God: for it is he that giveth thee power to get wealth, that he may establish his covenant which he sware unto thy fathers, as it is this day. (Deuteronomy 8:18)

I sent you to reap that whereon ye bestowed no labour: other men laboured, and ye are entered into their labours. (John 4:38)

For this cause shall a man leave his father and mother, and shall be joined unto his wife, and they two shall be one flesh. (Ephesians 5:31)

Rejoice not against me, O mine enemy: when I fall, I shall arise; when I sit in darkness, the Lord shall be a light unto me. (Micah 7:8)

A good man leaveth an inheritance to his children's children: and the wealth of the sinner is laid up for the just. (Proverbs 13:22)

Thy wife shall be as a fruitful vine by the sides of thine house: thy children like olive plants round about thy table. (Psalm 128:3)

Look, I go forward, but He is not there, And backward, but I cannot perceive Him; When He works on the left hand, I cannot behold Him; When He turns to the right hand, I cannot see Him. (Job 23:8–9)

that you may be sons of your Father in heaven; for He makes His sun rise on the evil and on the good, and sends rain on the just and on the unjust. (Matthew 5:45)

His mischief shall return upon his own head, and his violent dealing shall come down upon his own pate. (Psalm 7:16)

And it shall come to pass in that day, that his burden shall be taken away from off thy shoulder, and his yoke from off thy neck, and the yoke shall be destroyed because of the anointing. (Isaiah 10:27)

I beseech you therefore, brethren, by the mercies of God, that ye present your bodies a living sacrifice, holy, acceptable unto God, which is your reasonable service. And be not conformed to this world: but be ye transformed by the renewing of your mind, that ye may prove what is that good, and acceptable, and perfect, will of God. (Romans 12:1–2)

For which cause we faint not; but though our outward man perish, yet the inward man is renewed day by day. (2 Corinthians 4:16)

And be renewed in the spirit of your mind; (Ephesians 4:23)

Now it happened, as we went to prayer, that a certain slave girl possessed with a spirit of divination met us, who brought her masters much profit by fortune-telling. This girl followed Paul and us, and cried out, saying, "These men are the servants of the Most High God, who proclaim to us the way of salvation."

And this she did for many days. But Paul, greatly annoyed, turned and said to the spirit, "I command you in the name of Jesus Christ to come out of her." And he came out that very hour. (Acts 16:16–18)

"And I will restore to you the years that the locust hath eaten, the cankerworm and the caterpillar and the palmer worm, My great army which I sent among you. And ye shall eat in plenty and be satisfied, and praise the name of the Lord your God that hath dealt wondrously with you; and My people shall never be ashamed. And ye shall know that I am in the midst of Israel, and that I am the Lord your God, and none else; and My people shall never be ashamed. (Joel 2:25–27)

Praise and Worship

Deliverance from Demonic Foundational Stronghold

Prayer Points.

1. O Lord, I thank you for your power and ability to deliver me today, in the name of Jesus.
2. O Lord, I thank you that as I pray for my deliverance this day, you will hear me and set me free from all satanically and self-inflicted affliction, in the name of Jesus.
3. Lord Jesus, I thank you that in this deliverance program you will cancel every demonic programming going on in the second heaven against me, in the name of Jesus.
4. I receive power today, to pray through, in the name of Jesus.

5. I drink the blood of Jesus, from the well of salvation for my deliverance, healing and salvation, in the name of Jesus.
6. I destroy with the blood of Jesus, every demonic foundational stronghold in my life, in the name of Jesus.
7. Powers in my foundation response for my situation, die, in the name of Jesus.
8. O Lord, purge my foundation with your fire from any satanic pollution, in the name of Jesus.
9. Strongman of my foundation, loose your hold upon my life and die, in the name of Jesus.
10. I break any demonic and manipulative covenant in my foundation, in the name of Jesus.
11. Any foundational problem in life, die, in the name of Jesus.
12. Any satanic curses from my foundation troubling my life, break, in the name of Jesus.

Power against Marital Failure

13. Any satanic curses in my foundation affecting my marriage, break, in the name of Jesus.
14. Every evil projection from my foundation against my marital life, be destroyed with the fire of the Holy Ghost, in the name of Jesus.
15. I break any link to any demonic spiritual marriage, and I destroy the marriage certificate containing my name, in the name of Jesus.
16. Any spirit husband / wife, claiming ownership of my body, die, in Jesus name.

17. I divorce any spirit wife / husband I am unconsciously married to in the spirit realm, in the name of Jesus.

18. I neutralize the power of his / her semen in my body, blocking my physical ability to conceive, in the name of Jesus.

19. I command all the demonic children we have together in the spirit world crying against my earthly marriage, to die, in the name of Jesus.

20. I destroy all the properties of the spirit wife / husband in my possession, in the name of Jesus.

21. I break off every stronghold of the spirit wife / husband over my earthly marriage, in the name of Jesus.

22. My earthly marriage, receive deliverance by fire, in the name of Jesus.

23. I destroy any vow and covenant I have made with the spirit wife / husband, in the name of Jesus.

24. I command the physical and spiritual agent of the spirit wife / husband around me, to die, in the name of Jesus.

25. I use the blood of Jesus, to repair any physical and spiritual damage done to my earthly marriage by the spirit wife / husband, in the name of Jesus.

26. I command the spirit wife / husband to die by fire, in the name of Jesus.

27. This day, in the name of Jesus, I receive power, to conceive and deliver children in my earthly marriage, in the name of Jesus.

Destroying the Evil power behind
Frustration at Work / Business

28. Every witchcraft activities against my career/ business, die, in the name of Jesus.

29. Any power suppressing me from rising in my career / business, die, in the name of Jesus.

30. Any power preventing me from making great achievement in my career / business, die, in the name of Jesus.

31. Any evil pronouncement against my handy work, fall to the ground and die, in the name of Jesus.

32. I receive power of the Most High God to gain a meaningful employment, in this field (mention the kind of job), in the name of Jesus.

33. Any career / business destroying power assigned to destroy my career / business, I command death upon you, in the name of Jesus.

34. Holy Ghost arise and energize me for great achievement in my career / business this year, in the name of Jesus.

35. In this field / line of business I am, I decree, I will not fail like others, in the name of Jesus.

36. O Lord, awaken your favor upon my life to begin to work for me, in the name of Jesus.

37. I use the blood of Jesus to wash away any form of bewitchment on my head, causing disappointment in my life, in the name of Jesus.

38. By the power in the name of Jesus, I receive my rightful position in this field / business as the head, in the name of Jesus.

39. I shall not be hidden in this field / business, in the name of Jesus.

40. Any power assigned to cover me up and not to be noticed, die, in the name of Jesus.
41. O Lord, give me the wisdom to overtake my competitors in this field / business, in the name of Jesus.
42. Divine ideas that will advance me today, I possess you, in the name of Jesus.
43. I come out of the cages of collective captivity in my linage, in the name of Jesus.

Power Against Financial Failure

44. O Lord, make men work for me while reap their reward, according to your word in the book of John 4:38, in the name of Jesus.
45. I receive the divine power of God, to make wealth with ease, in the name of Jesus.
46. I receive the anointing of no struggle and be rich, in the name of Jesus.
47. Wisdom of the Lord, that made Abraham very rich in his own time, fall upon me, in the name of Jesus.
48. Anointing to be wealthy and still service God with all my heart, fall on me, in the name of Jesus.
49. Lord Jesus, recommend me to your father to make me a millionaire in Christ, in the name of Jesus.
50. I decree, in few days my testimony of becoming a multi-millionaire, shall be read worldwide, in the name of Jesus.
51. Forces of darkness working 24/7 to reduce me to nothing, you have failed, in the name of Jesus.
52. I reject the anointing of the borrower, I receive the anointing of a lender, in the name of Jesus.

53. When others are crying, O Lord my father, make me their deliverer like in the time of Joseph, in the name Jesus.

54. Covenants of Poverty of my father's and mother's house, clash and break to pieces, in the name of Jesus.

55. Every demon responsible for lack and poverty in my father's linage, die, in the name of Jesus.

56. Every demon responsible for lack and poverty in my mother's linage, die, in the name of Jesus.

57. As a child of the Most High God, from today, I decree that everything shall be possible for me and nothing shall be impossible, in the name of Jesus.

Power Against Home Breaker

58. Witchcraft coven in my territory responsible for failure, disappointment and poverty, you shall not locate my house, die, in the name of Jesus.

59. I declare and decree, my home is for Christ, therefore, no good thing shall we lack, in the name of Jesus.

60. Satanic angel of poverty on assignment against my home, receive blindness, in the name of Jesus.

61. Any power causing disunity in my home, die, in the name of Jesus.

62. Any power that is turning my home around for evil, you are a liar, die, in the of Jesus.

63. Spirit of the living God, make my home your place of abode, in Jesus name.

64. I command the destiny of my home, arise in the name of Jesus, and begin to walk in your divine purpose, in Jesus name.

65. Any power assigned to wreck my home, die, in the name of Jesus.

66. Any satanic pattern manifesting in my home, die, in the name of Jesus.

67. Powers that swallowed the happiness in my parent marriage, you will not succeed in mine, die, in the name of Jesus.

68. Powers that made my parent to struggle throughout their marital life, you will not succeed in mine, die, in the name of Jesus.

69. Strange man / woman focusing their attention on my marriage, receive blindness, in the of Jesus.

70. Any problem that came into my life because of this marriage, die, in the name of Jesus.

71. Any power attacking my destiny because of my marriage to my husband / wife, die, in the name of Jesus.

72. Any inherited sickness from my in-law's house because of my marriage to my wife / husband, die, in the name of Jesus.

Power Against Anti-Conception Spirit

73. My home shall be full of Children, in the name of Jesus Christ of Nazareth.

74. Every anti-conception spirit around us in my home, die, in the name of Jesus.

75. Every covenant of childlessness, causing miscarriages in my life, break, in the name of Jesus.

76. I decree by the power in the blood of Jesus, I shall be a mother / father of children, in the name of Jesus.

77. Any evil power that normally visit me at night, to terminate pregnancy whenever I am pregnant, the Lord rebuke you, die, in the name of Jesus.

78. Satanic curses of childlessness place upon of womb, break, in the name of Jesus.

79. Any satanic implantation in my womb preventing me from conceiving, dry up and die, in the name of Jesus.

80. I decree by this time of life, according to the word of God unto Sarah, I will conceive and give birth to my own children, in the name of Jesus.

81. Any power the enemies are using against my conception and delivery, die, in the name of Jesus.

82. I decree, I will not miss my divine opportunity for conception in this month, in the name of Jesus.

83. Blood of Jesus, mix with my blood and help me to conceive this month without any trouble, in the name of Jesus.

84. Parental curses affecting my ability to conceive, break, in the name of Jesus.

85. I move from this location of expectancy to the position of a mother / father of children, in the name of Jesus.

86. Any satanic covenant in my foundation, terminating pregnancy in my life, break, in the name of Jesus.

87. Any evil covenant with the dust of the earth against my conception, break, in the name of Jesus.

88. Powers using the dust of the earth to fight against my conception, die, in the name of Jesus.

89. My life begin to cooperate with the command of God, that says "go ye into the world and multiply" in the name of Jesus.

90. Dust of the earth release my children, in the name of Jesus.

91. Satanic covenant of get and lose in my life, die, in the name of Jesus.

92. Spiritual blockage of the powers of darkness, responsible for the delay in conception in my life, scatter, in the name of Jesus.

93. Powers that transport baby out of my womb, whenever I am pregnant, die, in the name of Jesus.

94. Spirit of miscarriage, loose your hold over my life, in the name of Jesus.

95. Powers calling baby out of my womb at the hours of the night, die, in the name of Jesus.

96. Powers punishing me for my past, enough is enough, die, in the name of Jesus.

97. Any evil deposit in my womb preventing pregnancy from staying, die, in the name of Jesus.

98. I command my husband semen to receive power to fertilize my eggs, in the name of Jesus.

99. Power of God, enter my being and make me fertile, in the name of Jesus.

100. Any covenant giving satanic powers right over my pregnancy, break, in the name of Jesus.

101. In the name of Jesus, I decree, I shall conceive in this month, in the name of Jesus.

102. Sing this song seven hot time "it shall be permanent, what the Lord has done for me, o yes, it shall be permanent"

103. Sing this song Seven hot times, "It shall not wither away, it shall not wither away, what the Lord has done for me, oh yes, it shall not wither away"

104. Powers of my in-law's house troubling my marriage and conception, die, in the name of Jesus.

105. Satanic persecutor of my father's house, die, in the name of Jesus.
106. Satanic persecutor of my mother's house, die, in the name of Jesus.
107. Powers crying against my marriage from my in-law's house, die, in the name of Jesus.
108. Men and women of darkness oppressing me at night during pregnancy, die, in the name of Jesus.
109. O Lord, make me a mother of children by your power in this year, in the name of Jesus.
110. Lord Jesus, over my life, ridicule my enemies this year, in the name of Jesus.
111. Marine covenant of childlessness, break in my life, in the name of Jesus.
112. Witchcraft covenant of childlessness, break in my life, in the name of Jesus.
113. Witchcraft bird that flies at the hours of the night to cause miscarriage in my life, die, in the name of Jesus.
114. Occultic powers that move around in the night to terminate my pregnancy, die, in the name of Jesus.
115. Powers that uses the blood to terminate my pregnancy, die, in the name of Jesus.
116. I break every evil hold over my pregnancy life, in the name of Jesus.
117. Any satanic animal that walk around in the night to terminate pregnancy in my life, die, in the name of Jesus.

Power Against Evil Dedication

118. Any power of evil dedication after my conception power, die, in the name of Jesus.

119. Any power I have been dedicated to by my forefathers, release me now, in the name of Jesus.

120. I command satanic hold over my life through evil dedication, to break, in the name of Jesus.

121. I move from the captivity of the power of evil, to freedom purchased through the blood of Jesus, in Jesus name.

122. I break off the covenant of the power of evil dedication in my life, in the name of Jesus.

123. O Lord, I dedicate my life to you, in the name of Jesus.

124. Lord Jesus, possess me alone, in the name of Jesus.

125. Idols of my father's house tormenting me because of my father's involvement in idolatry, die, in the name of Jesus.

126. Idols of my mother's house frustrating all my effort because of my mother's involvement in idolatry, die, in the name of Jesus.

Power to Renounce Membership with any Evil Association

127. I break every evil covenant between me and any evil association, in the name of Jesus.

128. Any witchcraft association demanding for my membership because of my last name, die, in the name of Jesus.

129. Any witchcraft association demanding for my membership because of my mother's linage, die, in the name of Jesus.

130. I break up with any occultic association, I have been enlisted to by my forefather and parents, in the name of Jesus.

131. I move out of darkness into the marvelous light of the son of God, in the name of Jesus.
132. Any Marine power calling my name for evil because I refuse to continue what my forefathers started, be silenced and die, in the name of Jesus.
133. I break loose from any witchcraft stronghold of my father's family, in the name of Jesus.
134. I vomit any food from witchcraft coven I have been fed with as a child, in the name of Jesus.
135. Any covenant that is giving any witchcraft association access to my life and home, break, in the name of Jesus.
136. I destroy any witchcraft pollution in my blood stream with the blood of Jesus.
137. Any darkness in any area of my life, be dispersed by the fire of God, in the name of Jesus.
138. I erase with blood of Jesus every witchcraft identification mark upon my body, in the name of Jesus.

Deliverance from Anti-Marriage Forces

139. Any power delaying the day of my marriage, your time is up, die, in the name of Jesus.
140. O Lord, send your ministering angel to locate the man you have prepared for me, and bring him now by fire, in the name of Jesus.
141. Satanic agreement entered into by my parent on my behalf, not allowing me to get married, die, in the name of Jesus.
142. Satanic mark of rejection place upon my body, making it difficult for me to get married, I erase you with the blood of Jesus.

143. Blood of Jesus, make me a bride / groom for the right man / woman in this year, in the name of Jesus.

144. Powers in possession of my marriage certification, die, in the name of Jesus

145. O Lord, command that man / woman you have made for me to come forth by fire, in the name of Jesus.

146. Powers responsible for fear in the life of the man for me, die, in the name of Jesus.

147. Any satanic veil covering my face and preventing God's will from locating me, be roasted by fire, in the name of Jesus.

148. Any power that stole my wedding gown / Suit in the dream, return it by fire, in the name of Jesus.

Power to divide your Personal Red Sea

149. I command any red sea situation in my life, dry up, in the name of Jesus.

150. Spirit of stagnancy at the point of breakthrough, die, in the name of Jesus.

151. Any power assigned to delay my advancement, die, in the name of Jesus.

152. I receive the thunder power of God, to bulldoze my way to breakthrough, in the name of Jesus.

153. Every spirit of lateness to the place of breakthrough, die, in the name of Jesus.

154. Jesus Christ of Nazareth, stretch forth your hand over my red sea today and dry it up, in the name of Jesus.

155. Powers standing between me and my promised land, back up and die, in the name of Jesus.

156. I receive the mantle of power like in the time of Elisha, to divide my Jordan, in the name of Jesus.

157. I command every stubborn pursuer behind me to drown in the red sea, in the name of Jesus.

158. Powers detaining me at the bank of my red sea, release me and die, in the name of Jesus.

Power Against Satanic Compass

159. Any evil authority using satanic compass to track me down, die, in the name of Jesus.

160. Any evil compass monitoring my movement, be destroyed by the blood of Jesus, in the name of Jesus.

161. Satanic Compass of the idol of my father's house, set in motion against me, be broken, in the name of Jesus.

162. I withdraw my name from the evil monitoring gadget of my village, in the name of Jesus.

163. I command the evil idol of my mother's house, using satanic compass to monitor my life, die, in the name of Jesus.

164. Blood of Jesus, shield me from satanic compass used to monitor me, in the name of Jesus.

165. Any evil compass from any river in my village used to monitor my progress, die, in the name of Jesus.

166. I command every witchcraft monitoring gadget used to monitor my progress, catch fire and burn to ashes, in Jesus name.

167. I shield my life from every demonic eye monitoring my progress, in the name of Jesus.

168. Every satanic monitoring eye monitoring the progress of my family, be blinded by fire, in the name of Jesus.

Destroying The power of Evil Resemblance

169. I reject any satanic look alike collecting my blessings, in the spiritual realm, in the name of Jesus.

170. I reject the power of satanic look alike in my father's lineage, in Jesus name.

171. I refuse my destiny to be fashioned after any satanic look alike, in the name of Jesus.

172. Any power claiming right over my destiny, because of satanic look alike, die, in the name of Jesus.

173. I refuse to continue the journey of satanic look alike in my life, in the name of Jesus.

174. I break all the evil connections, between me and any satanic look alike, in the name of Jesus.

175. Any evil power controlling my life because of satanic look alike, die, in the name of Jesus.

176. Any problem manifesting in life because of evil look alike, die, in the name of Jesus.

177. Any sickness manifesting in my life because of satanic look alike, die, in the name of Jesus.

178. I refuse to live my life after the life of a dead / living relative, in the name of Jesus.

179. Any evil load I am carrying because of satanic look alike, be destroyed by fire, in the name of Jesus.

180. Any evil decision manifesting in my life because of satanic look alike, die, in the name of Jesus.

181. Any satanic manipulation in my life because of satanic look alike, die, in the name of Jesus.

182. I shall not fulfill another person's destiny, in the name of Jesus.

183. Any battle coming into my life through my name, die, in the name of Jesus.

Destroying the Power of Internal Coffin

184. Any power shutting down my miracle from within me, die, in the name of Jesus.

185. Any power from my mother's house using me against myself, die, in the name of Jesus.

186. Ancient gate of my father's house crying against my rising, I shut you down, in the name of Jesus.

187. Every power of internal coffin inside of me attacking my potentials, die, in the name of Jesus.

188. Any strange voice speaking within me against my breakthrough, be silenced forever, in the name of Jesus.

189. O Lord, circumcise my heart with your blood, in the name of Jesus.

190. I refuse to work for the enemy against myself unconsciously, in the name of Jesus.

191. Any power within me cursing my head, die, in the name of Jesus.

192. Ancient powers of my father's house mounting evil walls against my life, die with your wall, in the name of Jesus.

193. I break down any satanic wall preventing me from moving forward in life, in the name of Jesus.

194. Any power in the spirit realm in-charge of my case file, die, in Jesus name.

195. Any power using the sun, moon and star to hinder my breakthrough, die, in the name of Jesus.

196. I capture back all the years, I have wasted on this earth with the blood of Jesus.

197. Any power killing good things in me before the maturity date, die, in the name of Jesus.

198. I shake off from my life the hand writing of the wicked, in Jesus name.

199. I refuse to labor for nothing, my life shall be meaningful, in Jesus name.

200. I rise up by the power that ascended Jesus up to heaven, in the name of Jesus.

201. I leave this location of weeping and regretting, I move up to the location of joy and fulfillment, in Jesus name.

202. Any spirit of almost there attacking my victory, success and breakthrough, die, in the name of Jesus.

203. Thou power of God, lift me from the dustbin of life to the palace, in the name of Jesus.

204. In the name of Jesus, I will no longer be comfortable with any position below my original, in the name of Jesus.

205. Any playful curses from my mother, father or friend attacking my destiny, break, in the name of Jesus.

Deliverance of the Head

206. I destroy any demonic pronouncement against my head by witchcraft powers, in the name of Jesus.

207. I destroy any parental negative word spoken against my head, in the name of Jesus.

208. Any evil judgement passed against my head from any witchcraft coven, fall to the ground and die, in the name of Jesus.

209. I nullify any evil effect of strange hands laid upon my head, in the name of Jesus.

210. Powers in charge of bad luck in my father's house, release my head, in the name of Jesus.

211. Blood of Jesus, deliver my head from any form of satanic manipulation, in the name of Jesus.
212. I break any satanic curse placed upon my head, in the name of Jesus.
213. I break any satanic covenant placed upon my head, in the name of Jesus.
214. I break every curse of shame and disgrace placed upon my head, by any satanic agent, in the name of Jesus.
215. I break any curse of failure and rejection placed upon my head, by satanic powers, in the name of Jesus.
216. Powers troubling my head, die, in the name of Jesus.
217. I erase any satanic mark placed upon my head, diverting good things away from me, in the name of Jesus.
218. My head, I command you to reject any form of bewitchment, in the name of Jesus.
219. Arrows of backwardness fired against my brain, backfire, in the name of Jesus.
220. Dark Powers of my mother's house attacking my head, die, in the name of Jesus.
221. I decree in the name of Jesus, my first shall not be the last, in the name of Jesus.
222. I break any covenant of backwardness formed with my head, in the name of Jesus.
223. I break any covenant of failure formed with my head, in the name of Jesus.
224. I break any covenant of stagnancy formed with my head, in the name of Jesus.
225. Fire of God, consume any satanic veil covering my head, in the name of Jesus.
226. Any evil sacrifice offered against my head, die, in the name of Jesus.

227. Powers using the weather to attack my head, die, in the name of Jesus.

228. Any demonic rain falling spiritually on my head, dry up, in the name of Jesus.

229. I withdraw my head from the altar of witchcraft, in the name of Jesus.

230. Lord Jesus, thank you for answered prayers, in the name of Jesus.

Deliverance of the Mind

231. Powers holding my mind captive, release me and die, in the name of Jesus.

232. Powers using my mind against me, die, in the name of Jesus.

233. Spirit of failure manifesting in my life through my thought, die, in the name of Jesus.

234. I circumcise my mind, with the blood of Jesus.

235. O Lord, deliver my mind with your blood, in the name of Jesus.

236. Powers caging my mind, release it and die, in the name of Jesus.

237. My mind hear the word of the living God, you will no longer cooperate with my enemies against me, in the name of Jesus.

238. O Lord, renew my mind with your power, in the name of Jesus.

239. My mind, I command you in the name of Jesus, stop abhorring evil thought against me, in the name of Jesus.

240. Blood of Jesus, sanitize my mind, in the name of Jesus.

241. My mind from today, dwell on the word of God, in the name of Jesus

242. Any satanic voice speaking to my mind, be silenced, in the name of Jesus.

243. Light of the living God, shine upon my mind, in the name of Jesus.

244. Spirit of doubt and fear dwelling in my mind, jump out and die, in the name of Jesus.

245. Spirit of slavery dwelling in my mind, die, in the name of Jesus.

246. Spirit of God, take control of my mind, in the name of Jesus.

247. My mind hear the word of the Lord, strange voices you shall not hear again from today, in the name of Jesus.

248. My mind shall not become the grave for good vision in my life, in the name of Jesus.

249. My mind, shall not be the grave of my divine prophecy, in the name of Jesus.

250. Every good thing lying dead on the altar of my mind, receive resurrection, in the name of Jesus.

251. Every thought of demotion in my mind against myself, die, in the name of Jesus.

252. Thank you, Lord, for answered prayer, in the name of Jesus.

Deliverance from Coffin Spirit

253. Any power ministering death into my life, die, in the name of Jesus.

254. Spirit of Suicide manifesting in my thought, die, in the name of Jesus.

255. Coffin spirit attacking my health, you are a liar, die, in the name of Jesus.

256. Spirit of depression attacking my health, die, in the name of Jesus.

257. Spirit of frustration attacking my life, die, in the name of Jesus.

258. I refuse to listen to any evil command of suicide from the devil, in the name of Jesus.

259. Powers calling me into untimely death, die, in the name of Jesus.

260. Coffin spirit responsible for untimely death in my family, loose your hold over my life, in the name of Jesus.

261. Coffin spirit hear the word of the Lord, Jesus died for me, that I might not die again, therefore, you coffin spirit come out and go straight in to the abyss, in the name of Jesus.

262. I destroy any spiritual coffin on assignment against me, in the name of Jesus.

263. O Lord, deliver me from coffin spirit pressurising me to kill myself, in the name of Jesus.

264. I decree from today, I shall no longer hear the voice of death but of the Holy Spirit, in the name of Jesus.

265. I drink the blood of Jesus from the well of salvation, for long life, good health, healing, deliverance and prosperity, in the name of Jesus.

266. Thank you Lord, for answered prayers, in the name of Jesus.

Silencing Witchcraft Cry

267. Powers crying day and night against my life, be silenced permanently by the blood of Jesus.
268. I cancel the evil effect of witchcraft cry over my life, in the name of Jesus.
269. Any witchcraft bird flying for my sake at the hours of the night, receive the arrows of death, in the name of Jesus.
270. Any satanic power, undertaking a deep sleep in order to harm me, sleep the sleep of death, in the name of Jesus.
271. I decree, I shall not be silenced by any witchcraft cry, in the name of Jesus.
272. Any power enchanting evil against my name, die, in the name of Jesus.
273. Any power divining evil against my name at the hours of the night, die, in the name of Jesus.
274. Powers calling my name for evil at the hours of the night, die, in the name of Jesus.
275. Powers keeping demonic vigil in order to harm me, sleep the sleep of death, in the name of Jesus.
276. Powers crying to cause confusion in my life, die, in the name of Jesus.
277. I nullify every occultic enchantment against me, in the name of Jesus.
278. O Lord, scatter their evil gathering against me, in the name of Jesus.
279. Any herbalist (Vodu man), hired for my sake, calling my name for evil, be silenced forever, in the name of Jesus.

280. Any incantation released into the wind against me, go back to your sender, in the name of Jesus.
281. My life, hear the voice of the Lord, you shall not hear the voice of any witchcraft cry, in the name of Jesus.
282. Father Lord, I thank you for answer to my prayers, in the name of Jesus

Deliverance from the Spirit of Wastage

283. I recover back all my wasted years, in the name of Jesus.
284. Any power that wants to keep me in perpetual bondage, release me and die, in the name of Jesus.
285. Where ever I have been sold to physically and spiritually, blood of Jesus, buy me back, in the name of Jesus.
286. I refuse to wander about without any achievement in life, in the name of Jesus.
287. Powers wasting my efforts, be wasted, in the name of Jesus.
288. Powers that have made demonic vow against my life, die with your vow, in the name of Jesus.
289. Powers assigned to keep me at one spot in life, loose your potency over my life and die, in the name of Jesus.
290. By the power in the Blood of Jesus, I recover back all my lost fertile ground in the custody of wicthcraft powers, in the name of Jesus.
291. Any area of my life in any witchcraft prison, be released by fire, in the name of Jesus.
292. I refuse my prince to become a slave in this life, in the name of Jesus.

293. Powers that want to change my gold to dust, you are a liar, die, in the name of Jesus.

294. Any power that want to use my life to obtain demonic promotion, die, in the name of Jesus.

295. I command every evil plan of household wickedness to waste my life, be frustrated by fire, in the name of Jesus.

296. Powers assigned to turn my day into night and my night into day, die, in the name of Jesus.

297. I refuse to be less than what God has created me to be, in the name of Jesus.

298. Powers exchanging destiny for more powers in my father's house, die, in Jesus name.

299. Lord Jesus, I thank you for answer to my prayer, in the name of Jesus

Suggested Hymns For Worship

NEARER MY GOD TO THEE

WHAT A FRIEND WE HAVE IN JESUS

BLESSED ASSURANCE JESUS IS MINE

TRUST AND OBEY

WHEN PEACE LIKE A RIVER

THROUGH THE LOVE OF OUR SAVIOR, ALL WILL
BE WELL

HOW GREAT THOU ART

THE GREAT PHYSICIAN NOW IS NEAR

HE TOUCHED ME

PRAISE MY SOUL THE KING OF HEAVEN

You Can Get Them From Your Local Hymn Books

About The book

Prayer that attract divine help from heaven is a prayer warfare book, written to assist people who desires to know how to confront satanic battles and have victory over them.

It is a book design by the Holy Ghost for modern day Christians, who are tired of been pushed around by evil powers of this age.

For we wrestle not against flesh and blood, but against principalities, against powers, against the rulers of darkness of the world, against spiritual wickedness in high places. (Ephesians 6:12). This prayer book is all about fighting these spiritual battles to enable you have a physical victory. In fighting battles, you sure need weapons, every prayer point in this book are spiritual arrows needed to fight your spiritual warfare. The bible says; (For the weapons of our warfare are not carnal, but mighty through God to the pulling down of strong holds). Casting down imaginations, and every high thing that exalteth itself against the knowledge of God, and bringing into captivity every thought to the obedience of Christ; (2 Corinthians 10:4–5).

In this prayer book, all the kill, die, destroy, cast down are warfare against the evil powers and our weapons of warfare include the use of the Name of Jesus, Blood of Jesus, stones of fire, thunder of God and generally the Word of God; which is life unto us. Pray using this book, your divine help from heaven will surely come in Jesus name.

Pastor Israel Oluwagbemiga was called into the Ministry as a Preacher, Teacher, Pastor and a Prophet of the Almighty God from 1997 in Nigeria. He has served in Various capacity in the Ministry. He went into full time Ministry 2001 in the District of Colombia. He is now the senior Pastor of Christ the Hope of Glory Mission in Grand Prairie, Texas.

He is a husband, father, an apostle and teacher of the word of God. Pastor Israel Oluwagbemiga, is an anointed man of God, full of wisdom, knownledge and understanding of the word of God, under the guidance of the Holy Spirit.

Christ The Hope Of Glory Mission Int'l
AKA (Balm Of Gilead Prayer And Miracle Ministries Int'l)
2100 S. Great Southwest Pkwy, Suite 503, Grand Prairie, TX 75051
☎ **682-3651803**